LA ROCHEFOUCAULD

W. G. MOORE

La Rochefoucauld

HIS MIND AND ART

OXFORD
AT THE CLARENDON PRESS
1969

Oxford University Press, Ely House, London W. 1

GLASGOW NEW YORK TORONTO MELBOURNE WELLINGTON
CAPE TOWN SALISBURY IBADAN NAIROBI LUSAKA ADDIS ABABA
BOMBAY CALCUTTA MADRAS KARACHI LAHORE DACCA
KUALA LUMPUR SINGAPORE HONG KONG TOKYO

Acknowledgements

LIKE most books which have been long in the making, this one owes much to many people. I am grateful to Henri Peyre and Richard Sayce for their patient and valued criticisms of an early draft; to Maurice Bowra for the generous and protracted loan of his facsimile of the Liancourt manuscript; to Jean Marchand and Antoine Adam for advice and encouragement; to the authorities of the *Revue de l'Histoire littéraire de la France*, the *Revue des Sciences Humaines*, and *French Studies* for publishing early drafts of three chapters; to students at Brandeis and Oxford who listened to the book in lecture form; to Henri Fluchère and Jacques Truchet, who gave much time to correcting a projected French version; and to Gilbert Highet, Humphrey Whitfield, Donald Russell, and Gaston Hall for advice and information.

Contents

ᚂᚉᚈ

A Note on Abbreviations

ΤϽℭϟ

THE name of the subject of this study being in itself a long one, and requiring frequent repetition, I have ventured to adopt its initial letters, as is common in professional circles, and to refer to the man known until his father's death in 1650 as François, Prince de Marcillac, and after that date as François, Duc de La Rochefoucauld, by the capital letters LR. (In a case of similar difficulty, Kierkegaard is referred to throughout Mr. Lowrie's long biography as K.)

LR's chief work is usually called the *Maximes*. I so italicize the work when referring to the book published first in 1665, but I refer in roman type to the kind of epigram which LR has made famous as Maximes.

I refer to the first edition of 1665 as A, to the Dutch edition of 1664 as H, and to the Liancourt manuscript, of which parts are said to be in LR's own hand, as L. Unaccompanied page references are to the second printing of the 'Pléiade' edition, in 1957. Therein the Maximes are numbered consecutively throughout, except for the nineteen *Réflexions diverses*, to which I refer as *RD*, with their own numbers.

RHLF   *Revue de l'histoire littéraire de la France.*
NRF   *Nouvelle Revue Française.*
Br. minor   *Pensées et opuscules*, ed. Brunschvicg (Hachette).

1. Introduction

To those who read literature for pleasure LR is a classic, in the strict sense of an author whose reputation is established. His status as a writer is admitted in all respects save one. He is edited, in cheap editions, in school editions, in translation, in anthology. But he is not studied. Of course his work is set for study in public examinations and appears in histories of French literature, but no detailed study of his work has appeared within the last fifty years. Recent biographies, a few articles, a couple of theses, these are almost all that a student can find of help.

French neglect of French classical writers will one day have a thesis all to itself. Even Sainte-Beuve had to apologize for returning to problems which he found in writers about whom all was presumed to have been said. The classical group of seventeenth-century authors suffered particularly from this, owing to the official view—going back to Nisard and even to La Harpe—that the Cartesian basis of French classicism being clear, problems of aesthetic and imagination did not arise. No systematic study of Molière's comedy on aesthetic principles exists. Only slowly have Sorbonne professors learned from actors that classical plays have certain laws and norms and forms. But the production of research theses on seventeenth-century literature is still minute when compared with theses on nineteenth- and twentieth-century literature. Even now we can know more about Fontenelle and Saint-Simon than we can about Mme de Sévigné, Mme de La Fayette and La Rochefoucauld.

Only when particular investigations have reached a certain point shall we know what the central group of French writers in their classical age were really saying. It may prove to be something very different from what we call classical. The qualities of generality, order, rationality which we are invited to see in classical literature tell us in effect little about it. Individuality, as we find it in Rabelais or in Rousseau, is not found, but this absence is not due to any literary theory so much as to the fact that in the seventeenth century the individual had no right to an opinion just because it was his own; he had to fit it into a hierarchy of authorities in comparison with which an individual was insignificant. Bossuet once defined a heretic as a man who 'has an opinion'.

If one does not write in a personal and individual way, how else can one write than impersonally? If one is not ruled by authority, what other basis can there be for opinion than reason? The features of French classicism turn out on close scrutiny to be aspects of seventeenth-century ways of thinking and tell us little about the aesthetic or the imagination of some great writers.

La Rochefoucauld is surely a case in point. He can hardly be read with full understanding, since no elucidation of his work exists. The 'Grands Écrivains' edition is a mine of information, and so in a smaller way are the 'Pléiade' editions. But what scholar has used them, more than to quote an odd reference, or to support an opinion?

How were the *Maximes* written? What was the equipment, mental, cultural, moral, of their author? What is their relation to the Augustinian circle in which they were produced? These questions await an answer, and some of them have never been asked. How many readers of LR have been concerned to read him without prejudice, and to examine how far he deserves his reputation? Since Sainte-Beuve I could name only one or two. A recent doctoral thesis analysed the style and even the sound effects found in his writing. Since the chief sounds were said, without evidence, to convey cynicism, one could not avoid the suspicion that the author had started out with an impression she had been glad to confirm.

I do not claim that LR was not a cynic, but I do contend that the question should be approached with some objectivity and care for the rules of evidence. To any who have followed his tortuous career through the Fronde, in the government of Poitou, in the struggle against Mazarin and the royal power, it would be surprising if this intelligent and unfortunate man were not embittered. Not only so, but his acute scrutiny of the behaviour of what, after all, were only certain groups in the society around him, should not make us assume that when he writes *l'homme* or *on*, he is to be believed about the nature of all men everywhere. In one sense the *Maximes* may be read as the autopsy of a dying class. The surprising thing about them is not the frequency of cunning, hypocrisy, trickery, and selfishness, but the discernment and penetration into other things, the interest that LR shared with Pascal, for example, in questions of the mind, in its force and its variety, in intuition, common sense, and judgement. LR can be read as a most intelligent disciple of Montaigne, but this too has never been worked out.

Nor has scholarship seriously come to grips with the technical problems of his work. Editions and manuscripts have been listed and arranged by bibliographers, but to what use have they been put? Is it not common to speak of his book as a collection of maxims? It is much more than that. A Sorbonne professor has gone so far as to claim that he was not a creative writer. One isolated attempt has been made by a historian of modern ideas to connect LR with developments in the Enlightenment, and to see in him a forerunner of Bentham. Are these things simply a matter of conjecture? Nobody seems to have explored possible connections with the kindred spirit who was his exact contemporary, Hobbes. Is it not possible in this, as in other sciences, to assess the evidence and to obtain results, so that we do not have each critic saying what he likes regardless of evidence? LR exposes the weakness of the science of literary history. It is this sort of impasse of which Gide once wrote: 'ces lacunes seraient inadmissibles en zoologie, . . . nous les excusons en littérature, domaine de la confusion, de l'hésitation et de l'à-peu-près.'

This is not to say that erudition has entirely neglected LR. If attempts at elucidation are lacking, study of the documentary evidence, concerning both the man and his work, has been active and has provided a foundation for inquiry. The abundant archive material has been sifted by Émile Magne; the bibliographical confusion has been attacked, and largely cleared up, by Jean Marchand. The voluminous papers dealing with the salon of Mme de Sablé, known as the Portefeuilles Vallant, have been investigated by M. Ivanov. The background of LR's life has of course benefited from the new study of the Fronde, particularly as practised by Mr. Kossman and Roland Mousnier. So all is ready. The next step is to apply the new data to the study of the text of LR's masterpiece.

Here we meet confusion again. In the textbooks LR figures as the author of two works, not only of one. Could one more effectively obscure the fact that one of these works is a tract of doubtful value, both historical and literary, and the other a masterpiece of world literature, a book of which Nietzsche said that LR made the Greeks look like children? If LR had written only the *Mémoires* I do not think he would claim any space in a history of French literature. The *Mémoires* are well written, acute, biased of course, but without any superior talent. LR's servant Gourville seems to me to have done almost as well. But as a source book for the *Maximes*, as the raw material that would serve him in thinking out problems of conduct, the *Mémoires* are invaluable. It is time that they were used as such.

Where then should we start? All study of epigrams must take account of two factors. Epigram is the reverse of transparent; one of its objects is to conceal its origins and its particular reference, in order to suggest a general judgement. Yet every epigram is born of restricted personal experience, no man has ever been more than an individual. We have therefore two things to study: the experience which has gone to the making, and the art which has succeeded in concealing. Some may think that this is going too far, violation of the author's privacy, which he has deliberately attempted to preserve. So I think, as a general reader. But as a scholar, I can only resist misinterpretation and misrepresentation by knowing what really went on. Therefore any clues as to the formation of epigram must be carefully examined. The author's deliberate actions with regard to his text must be accounted for. We must know where, and what, he has altered, published, withdrawn from publication.

The basic facts are simply told. The standard text was set up by the author himself in 1678. It excluded many Maximes already published. It altered many others. Are we to say that these acts and changes have no importance? Scholars have implied this, if they have not actually said it. To suggest that emendation of the text consisted of insertion or omission of words like *peut-être* or *toujours* is to imply this.

Much of the standard text can therefore be read with the help of the first edition. How far can we go behind the editions? To this question we can give a precise answer. M. Marchand has listed and collated no less than fourteen different manuscripts of the *Maximes*, of which the present whereabouts of three is not known, and of which two bear the author's own hand. None of these fourteen offers the text from which the first edition was printed. The later editions, as M. Marchand points out, were established from the earlier, not from any of the extant manuscripts.

To sum up: of the 641 Maximes we find in the current editions, about three hundred were first published in 1665. In modern editions these are divided: they occupy most of the first three hundred of the serial numbering, and seventy-six of the section 'Maximes supprimées', items which LR withdrew after his first edition. For many of these, early drafts exist in the manuscripts. Ancillary material is found in LR's letters, in copies of replies received when LR circulated his drafts, and in a series of nineteen *Réflexions diverses*, seven of which were published in 1731 and the rest in 1863. Of the date of these nothing is known; some of them mention events of the late seventies, so were probably written in the last years of LR's life, between 1677 and 1680.

The chief problem posed for literary history by this material concerns the origin and early forms of the kind of epigram which is called a Maxime. This will be discussed later as a form of art, but it may be said now that to speak of all the items in the editions just mentioned as Maximes is incorrect, and that LR himself never did this. He was careful to give to his first edition a triple title: *Réflexions ou Sentences et maximes morales*. Many of what we refer to as Maximes are really '*réflexions*', if we adhere to the usual meaning of *réflexion* as a series of comments or definitions, of undetermined length. The Maxime is an epigram, a single thought reduced to its most concentrated expression. Many problems need not have been raised if this elementary distinction had been kept in mind.

It is, I suggest, of some importance to insist that LR is not only the author of epigrams. Some of his finest writing is not in any strict sense epigram at all. The famous item on *amour-propre*, for instance, is of course not an epigram. Nor is it written in the style of epigram.

In the manuscripts it is one of many such reflections, concise indeed but not aimed entirely at brevity. From many such reflections Maximes seem to come, as if the course of reflection would at some point coalesce into a global or cogent phrase which would express or suggest that to which the reflection had been tending. In this sense we may think of reflections as the ground and preparation for the Maxime. But this does not mean that once the Maxime has been discovered the rest of the reflection may be abandoned. We are dealing with two kinds of literary expression. Some truths can be approached best in the one form, some in the other. To call LR a writer of Maximes is not therefore strictly correct, since he also wrote *réflexions* which are among his finest writing. It might be best to call him by the French word *moraliste*, something different from a moralist, not concerned with ethical issues only but with a picture of human behaviour which shall throw into relief its paradox, its complexity, in a word which shall suggest the irony of the human condition. All study of LR culminates here. Far from being the secretary of a group, as is often thought, he is a writer not only of great imaginative power, but a man who took writing seriously, who spent time on rewriting, on patiently seeking the phrase, or even the word, that would illuminate his point. This is far from the usual picture of a cynic who happened to have the gift of picturesque brevity. In fact study of LR does not enforce the notion of the cynic; it increases our respect for the writer. Inverting Pascal's phrase we may say : *on s'attendait à trouver un homme, et on trouve un auteur.*

The best single example on which to test the foregoing arguments is perhaps provided by numbers 17 and 18 in the standard editions of the *Maximes*. They concern the quality of moderation, an aristocratic and indeed a military virtue, the quality of a man in possession of power, yet strong enough to refrain from the full exercise of that power. It was a case that must have been both discussed and exemplified during the Fronde. If we turn to A, the first authorized edition, we find not two but five Maximes on the subject. Of these, two were removed by the author from his second edition, and one was placed considerably further on in the collection. To read therefore what he first published we must read together these Maximes: 17, 18, 293, 565, 566. This in itself gives quite a different appearance to his *sentences*. Many of the epigrams suggest fairly long thought, chiefly on memories of civil war. It is curious to find this recalled in conditions which must have been the very opposite, the polite and select society of a Paris salon, from which such dangerous subjects as politics and religion were barred.

If now we pass to study of the manuscripts we find all five items together in the Dutch edition of 1664 (H). Is there not therefore a prima facie case for thinking that LR (whether before or after discussions in the salon) took care to write down some reflections on the matter, revised these on several occasions, and finally succeeded in presenting them to his first readers as separate disconnected observations, of a laconic nature, which by being separated, and not linked to a general argument, were enabled to strike the more sharply on a reader necessarily unprepared for each one?

For convenience I append the text of H, so that users of the standard edition may compare it with their own:

La modération dans la bonne fortune n'est que la crainte de la honte, qui suit l'emportement ou la peur de perdre ce que l'on a. C'est le calme de notre humeur, adoucie par la satisfaction de l'esprit; c'est aussi la crainte du blâme et du mépris, qui suivent ceux qui s'enivrent de leur bonheur; c'est une vaine ostentation de la force de notre esprit; et enfin pour la définir intimement la modération des hommes dans leurs plus hautes élévations est une ambition de paraître plus grands que les choses qui les élèvent.

Qui ne rirait de cette vertu et de l'opinion qu'on a conçue d'elle? Elle n'a garde, ainsi qu'on le croit, de combattre et de soumettre l'ambition, puisque jamais elles ne se peuvent trouver ensemble, la modération n'étant véritablement qu'une paresse, une langueur et un manque de courage; de manière qu'on peut justement dire que la modération est la bassesse de l'âme, comme l'ambition en est l'élévation.

Study of this passage, and comparison with the Maximes on moderation which appear in the standard text, suggest that the material of the earlier Maximes has come to us in various forms, and that careful collation may tell us something of the origins of epigram. To do this adequately on the case before us I think that we should have in mind the passages found in the manuscript L, sometimes called the *manuscrit original*. They are numbered 70, 71, and 77 ('Pléiade' edition, pp. 356–7). No. 70 states that moderation is a matter for laughter since it is no more than an absence of ambition. No. 71 reproduces the first sentence quoted above from H, concerning moderation as fear of public exposure. No. 77 starts with the same words as No. 71: *La modération dans la bonne fortune* . . ., and reproduces lines 3–9 of the passage just quoted from H.

Here then is our evidence. What does it allow us to conclude? In the first place surely that the connected passages precede the isolated statements, that the Maximes proceed from reflections. This is entirely natural: to suppose the opposite would be extraordinary. Secondly, if this be granted, then the longer and more connected statement is older, and earlier, than the isolated Maxime. I find nothing surprising about this either. It is what one would expect and what one finds in such literary material. It is borne out by the fact (if extra evidence be needed) that L certainly preceded A as A certainly preceded O, the standard text. So, underlining the obvious, we may imagine LR reflecting on a matter of experience, perhaps discussing it with a group of friends, then writing down the conclusions to which he came, which amounted to redefining in the light of particular experience a quality of behaviour. The next stage was to separate his assertions from each other, so that they have the effect of distinct and independent statements, not of parts of a paragraph. The final stage, seen in our present editions, is to carry this process to its logical end by splitting up the already separated reflections, so that they should not get in each other's way (so to say) by being read consecutively. This means that what we now read as numbers 17, 18, and 293, if they are to be studied, must be thought of as stemming from a common original, which we can approach by adding two of the Maximes withdrawn by their author after his first edition. But if this filiation seems obvious, let us remark one implication which has not been noticed. Both H and L give us, in this as in many cases, states of later Maximes, yet they do not always give us the same state. Keeping to our example of the passages on moderation, and considering L and H in the light of each other, which of the two would seem to be nearer to a first draft? Some who think of L as LR's oldest surviving version of his thoughts would be hard put to it to explain why, in the course of a short reflection, he repeats a formula such as *la modération dans la bonne fortune*. Again, comparing such statements as these two:

(*a*) Qui ne rirait de la modération . . .
and (*b*) Qui ne rirait de cette vertu . . .

would not the second seem in the more logical position, as comment on a quality already defined, rather than introduction to a series of definitions? To assume L as in this case prior to H is to imagine someone, certainly not the author, transposing the thought of L into the more logical and connected framework of H. Is it not much easier and more sensible to think of both the Dutch

Corrigenda

p. 11, note 1, line 2: *for* edition *read* editions
    line 3: *for* Truchet Garnier *read* Truchet (Garnier)

p. 23, line 12: *missing page reference is* 25–6
    line 13: *for* L'humilite *read* L'humilité
    line 17: *for* premeir *read* premier
    line 21: *for* l'humilte *read* l'humilité
           for baissez *read* baissés

p. 40, line 9: *for* assiégés *read* assiegés

p. 59, line 9 from bottom: *for* crœu *read* cœur

p. 94, line 7: *for* Parado lis *read* Paradol is

printer and the scribe of L working on a version older than either of them? The Dutchman transcribes it and the scribe of L, possibly the master himself, alters it. If this is sound, the version behind H should perhaps be treated as the oldest extant state of the material that went into the making of the *Maximes*.[1]

[1] Since the above was written three scholars have committed themselves to the view that H is a clumsy re-writing of L. See the recent edition of the *Maximes* by Truchet Garnier, and Secretan (T.F.M.) and G. Laffond in *Revue de l'histoire littéraire de la France*; 1966, pp. 296-305.

2. The Early Documents

I HOPE that the method of our inquiry is now becoming clear. Study of LR's thoughts on 'moderation' suggests that the process of coining an epigram was long, slow, tentative. Reflections which are not yet in the form of epigram seem to have been a basis on which to work in concentrating and isolating thoughts that were first written down continuously. Is the case we have chosen an exception? I think not. Analysis of the Maximes on clemency (15, 16) and those on justice (78, 578, 579, 580) would bring us to the same conclusion. In all three of these cases the oldest state of the material would seem to be preserved by a pirated edition, decried by LR himself and thought by scholars to be of less importance than the manuscript usually called the original. Let us therefore look at these early versions and see to what use they may be put in the study of the finished Maximes.[1]

In 1879 an expert in Elzevirs, M. Willems, discovered a volume with the title *Sentences et maximes de morale*, printed at the Hague by Jean and Daniel Steucker, without date of either *privilège* or *achevé*, in 1664. The same booksellers (for they practised both trades) printed issues about the same time of the first editions of Bassompierre's *Mémoires* and of Brantôme. M. Willems assumed that they procured one of the Paris manuscript copies supposed to circulate within a restricted circle. Their printer seems to have made many more mistakes than

---

[1] For details see *RHLF*, 1952, pp. 417–24.

any other scribe working for LR could have done. He printed *interpidité, d'eclin* (for *destin*), *semences* (for *sentences*), *vous* (for *nous*), *superflues* (for *superficielles*), *pitie* (for *piété*) and probably *justice* (for *jugement*). It would seem to me unlikely that he was capable or desirous of making other and far-reaching alterations to his text. (I admit that an intelligent editor may have been served by a bad compositor, whose blunders he did not bother to correct.) Those who think that H is a botched-up adaptation of L must assume that the editor was clever enough to put together separated reflections on the same subject. This seems to me impossible, and entirely without supporting evidence. The agreement, indeed, between L and H is considerable, so much so that we might think of the manuscript that served the Dutch printer as having been constituted about the same time as L, that is in 1663. To take a single case, both documents give for No. 44, on the strength and weakness of the mind, the same formula: *La faiblesse de l'esprit est mal nommée.* It is interesting to have this hint that the Maxime may have sprung from an observation of the connection between poor physique and poor intelligence. At times, however, the text of H reads as rougher and more elementary than that of L. It has *rien n'est impossible* for L's *rien n'est impossible de soi.* . . . It puts together reflections which are separated in L. Unless, again, we assume a deliberate design to do this (for which no evidence exists), then we must think of an early draft containing statements which later were divided.

The closest study of the content of H has been the work of Dr. Brix, who, in his dissertation of 1913, counted no less than 22 items in A, which cover 21 items in L and only 10 in H. His findings have only once been challenged and rarely acknowledged. The content of a single paragraph in H is often widely separated in L but almost contiguous in A.

It is a pity that M. Willems referred to the paragraphs of H as *Maximes*. Many of them would be more properly called reflections, on the way, we might say, to becoming 'Maximes. To call the famous pages on *amour-propre* a Maxime' is to discredit the meaning of the word. Willems might have told us that in H these pages are followed by others, so that they present what might be called a short essay on the subject, written no doubt in view of reducing still further certain pointed observations. To bring home, for example, the effect of *amour-propre* in love he imagines a lover

agité de la rage où l'a mis un visible oubli ou infidélité découverte conjurer le ciel et les enfers contre sa maîtresse et néanmoins aussitôt qu'elle s'est présentée et que sa vue a calmé la fureur de ses mouvements, son ravissement rend cette beauté innocente; il n'accuse plus que lui-même, il condamne ses condamnations, et par cette vertu miraculeuse de l'amour-propre il ôte la noirceur aux actions mauvaises de sa maîtresse et en sépare le crime pour en charger ses soupçons. (Éd. Pléiade, p. 324.)

It is a pity to call this a Maxime, with which it has very little to do. It is a vignette from real life, or from the theatre. Anyone who takes the trouble to read it in the light of Act II, scene vi of *Dom Garcie de Navarre*, played at Chantilly and Versailles and Paris in the autumn and winter of 1663, will consider the writing of the *moraliste* as comparable to that of the dramatist.

The Dutch edition should not in fact be used only to establish priorities and changes of phrasing. It is a proof of what the world lost when LR decided to convert his reflections into epigrams. The keen observation of detail, the excellent reporting, these and similar graces may still be read in H and in No. 563 of the standard edition. They are among the fine writing of their age.

Yet H also contains evidence of the attraction of the single pregnant phrase, of the urge to reduce language to its barest outline, of the cult of what in all ages has been pleasing—*abbreviatio*. This gift LR seemed to feel that he possessed, and to it we owe the finest successes of his genius. One reason, perhaps, why the Dutch edition angered him was that it made public a reflection on this precise point, which he would never agree to publish (No. 505):

Dieu a mis des talents différents dans l'homme, comme il a planté des arbres différents dans la nature, en sorte que chaque talent, ainsi que chaque arbre, a sa propriété et son effet qui lui sont particuliers. De là vient que le poirier le meilleur du monde ne saurait porter les pommes les plus communes, et que le talent le plus excellent ne saurait produire les mêmes effets du talent le plus commun; de là aussi vient qu'il est aussi ridicule de vouloir faire des sentences, sans avoir la graine en soi, que de vouloir qu'un parterre produise des tulipes, quoi qu'on n'y ait point semé d'oignons.

The manuscript known as Liancourt (L) is our next important source for the early state of the earliest reflections of LR. M. Marchand has described it for us as *un petit in-folio en papier, à la reliure souple de parchemin blanc, ornée de filets et de fleurons dorés, légèrement détériorée,* and his facsimile allows us to study not only the phrasing but the handwriting, four passages being thought by the experts to be in LR's own hand, a total of sixteen pages out of ninety-one.[1]

The paragraphs of this document are not numbered, but opposite many of them is a small letter which would identify the subject and serve to compose a register for quick reference. Comparing the text with that of the Dutch edition, it would seem that LR had copied many of his entries from such a manuscript as that which served the Dutch printer. Many others he had divided

[1] On all this see Éd. Pléiade, pp. 341–2, and J. Marchand, *Les Manuscrits des 'Maximes' de La Rochefoucauld,* tirage à part du *Bulletin du Bibliophile,* 1935.

and separated. But clearly this process had not gone
nearly so far as in the draft given to Barbin for printing
in 1665. A curious sample of this is No. 9, which in both
H and L had this additional sentence: *La charité a seule
le privilège de dire tout ce qui lui plaît et de ne blesser jamais
personne* (L, 164). Does it not influence our judgement of
this Maxime to know that it was not an isolated reflection
on the passions and their tendency to hurt other people
when put into words, but a comparison with the exercise
of a Christian virtue? This reference was one of several
that LR excised in 1665, and which appear in the early
drafts and in the posthumous papers. It suggests an
ambiance of religion (not surprising in the shadow of
Port Royal) which has gone to the making of Maximes,
but which convention would not allow to appear in their
public formulation.

3. The First Edition

꿍

Les premières éditions ont en général une physiono-
mie qui n'est qu'à elles, et apprennent je ne sais quoi
sur le dessein de l'auteur que les autres, augmentées
et complétées ne disent plus.

WHEN we recall that this opinion was thrown out *en
passant*, before the days of bibliographies and critical
editions, it seems astonishing that Sainte-Beuve should
have the prescience to anticipate the minute attention to
the life of a great book which nowadays is taken for
granted. Of few great works is the remark more true than
of the *Maximes*. The slim volume which came off the
presses of Claude Barbin on 27 October 1664, and bears
the date of 1665, seems to have been sold so quickly
that three *contrefaçons* and a second edition appeared within a year. '*Ce chien de Barbin*', as Mme de Sévigné called
him, no doubt in jest, seems to have had a keener eye
for new writing than his rival Charles Sercy, LR's first
publisher, who had not encouraged him to offer anything else in the style of the pages on *amour-propre* which
he had printed in the *Recueil* of 1662. Dismayed, we
are told, by a scornful remark to the effect that these
now famous pages were '*galimatias*' (as indeed they
seemed, in the context of *précieux* light verse), LR was
probably most reluctant to publish at all. He had consented to collaborate with a few friends and refers in a
letter (undated) to '*notre volume*'. But as an aristocrat he
did not relish becoming an author, for money, even
though he seems to have been constantly hard up. He

writes to his friend and intended collaborator Jacques Esprit (a letter dated by the 'Pléiade' editors 1660, and by him only *le 24 octobre*) as follows: *La honte me prend de vous envoyer des ouvrages. Tout de bon, si vous les trouvez ridicules, renvoyez-les moi, sans les montrer à Mme de Sablé* (Éd. Pléiade, p. 604). So it was probably only the appearance of the pirated Dutch edition that forced his hand, and made him consign to cold print those many reflections on which he had for some years worked patiently. Manuscript variants are numerous enough for us to imagine without undue fantasy a care for detail and a dissatisfaction with the apparently unimportant word which remind us of Balzac's hesitation over figures and names.

Psychologically, therefore, an edition of the *Maximes* may well have been a more important new departure for him than for most writers. Cold print forced him to decide between variants, to have a larger public in mind than the friends who had received written copies, to make up his mind about his arrangement of thoughts on many subjects. The fact that when his book had proved a success he removed from a second edition no less than 75 items from the first indicates either his hesitation or his perfectionist scruples, or both.

From our point of view the study of LR's first edition of the *Maximes* amply justifies Sainte-Beuve's remark. Although reprinted by M. Marescot in 1869, the volume is not widely known and has never to my knowledge been studied. It deserves study on several grounds. If LR be thought of as the inventor of the French classical epigram, then this is the point at which the process starts, for the public. It is valuable for us to know how tentative were LR's beginnings, how unsure he was of judging public taste, how far he was prepared to go, how closely he kept to the taste of the salons where his Maximes had been produced.

Of the original edition of a famous work several questions can be asked. We may study its relation to the version we know, which gives us a chance to compare the first 'leap', so to say, into print with the mature decision of the author who has had time to judge the effect of his words on his public. No less worthy of study is the relation of the first printed text to the earliest drafts preserved by the manuscripts. In a work of form, such as a collection of epigrams, the variants will tell us of the gradual emergence or achievement of the form. Did we not have the abandoned drafts we should not, perhaps, suspect how hard was the artist's task in reaching perfect or adequate expression of new material. The final text does not tell us whether the Maxime, in the strict sense, meaning that soul of wit which is found in brevity, was a sudden illumination or the result of a process of trial and error. Most discussions of the *Maximes* do not raise the point.

So that a final question about a first edition of epigrams would be: how far has the process come? Assuming that at some early stage the artist discovered that out of the reflection may arise the single gem of expression, we may imagine that he was faced with the choice between publication of reflections and publication of Maximes. In the case of the volume we are now studying the answer is not the less illuminating for seeming obvious. LR decided, in making up his edition for the printer, to include both the Maximes and the reflections, probably for the quite simple reason that he had not enough of either category to make a book by itself. Also no doubt because some subjects give rise to reflections and others to Maximes. Thus the volume opens with what one might call a three-page essay on *amour-propre*. Nothing could be, in form, more different from a Maxime. Is this why the item was withdrawn from the second edition? Probably not, as I have suggested. Nor did it stand

alone: many other reflections extend to ten or twenty
lines. Some of these remained until 1678, when the
standard text was established (those, for instance, on
courage (215) and on grief (233)). But in A they are
numerous: instead of the four lines of 88, also on *amour-
propre*, A has twenty-six; No. 65 has twelve in place of
the present two; No. 254 has fourteen, now reduced to
six. Clearly therefore A shows us a process in being, half
completed. The process of 'chiselling', as it has been
called, has in 1665 gone only half way: in many cases LR
has in later editions carried it considerably further.

Once this point has been established, we are free to
admire the fact that the most interesting formal feature
of A is the number of reflections which have already, by
1665, reached their point of ultimate decision. The perfect epigram is in the first edition already achieved, a
fact which not only contributed to the rapid sale of the
volume but has blinded the attention of scholars to the
presence of material that cannot with any accuracy be
called epigram. This point hardly stands in need of illustration, since readers will recall their personal favourites.
One thinks of the comparison of the sun and death (26),
of the candle and the forest fire (276), of the description
of old men as consoled by giving good advice for their
inability to give bad example (93), or of desire for praise
as the source of praise (146). But these are a few among
the many. They show a brilliance comparable to that
seen in a perfect sonnet, or in a purple passage of modern
prose. By their occurrence in A they throw serious
doubts on the notion of Victor Cousin that LR was
merely the secretary, noting the decisions of the group.
They are unthinkable without the patience, as well as
the inspiration, of genius.

One would like to know how these marvels of speech
came to be, the sort of thing which, say, the first drafts
of *The Prelude* tell us of the genesis of Wordsworth's

poem. But the extant manuscripts contain no first version of the best of these Maximes. There exists no single manuscript of which we can say that it is the basis of the first edition. The formulation in A is in many cases that of L, which some please to call '*le manuscrit original*'. But of the order this cannot be said. Either LR was dissatisfied with the order of L or he had another manuscript in front of him. In some places the sequence of A is that of H, the Dutch edition, so we may think of LR as working on a manuscript similar to that used for the pirated edition which forced LR to publish. But there are no less than thirty reflections in A which are found in no manuscript, and which we may think of as having been worked out during the preparation of A.

Another obvious formal feature of the text of A is a certain directness of expression which has later been smoothed out. The phrases are more natural, less artistic, than they later became. A good example is the text of what we now read as No. 24:

Les grands hommes s'abattent et se démontent à la fin par la longueur de leurs infortunes : cela fait bien voir qu'ils n'étaient pas forts quand ils les supportaient, mais seulement qu'ils se donnaient la gêne pour le paraître et qu'ils soutenaient leurs malheurs par la force de leur ambition et non pas par celle de leur âme ; enfin à une grande vanité près les héros sont faits comme les autres hommes.

The passage is interesting for two other reasons. First, that the word *gêne* has not its modern sense, but rather that of 'torment': H actually spells the word *gehenne*. Second, that the final phrase, which has the ring and challenge of a Maxime, is textually found in the prose version by Jacques Esprit, published in 1678 on the basis of notes which he must have taken at the same time as LR. Here, as so often, we are left in the dark as to the actual origin of the observation. Both writers may be registering the decision of the salon; either may be giving us a formula invented by the other. LR does at least suggest the origin of the general reflection, in a form which reminds us of his own account in the *Mémoires* of meeting his friends who had been kept long in prison by Richelieu.

This same directness of utterance, at times approaching violence, must have been shocking in a salon. Compare the later inoffensive ending of No. 28 with this: *l'envie est une fureur qui nous fait toujours souhaiter la ruine du bien des autres*. A frequent feature of A is an absence of qualification, and thus a vigour and directness of approach which we now miss. Thus No. 7 has no *peut-être*, No. 10 no *presque*, No. 146 no *d'ordinaire*, No. 53 no *seule* and *avec elle*. After all, it is more immediate to say *l'intérêt seul produit notre amitié* than to say *néanmoins c'est l'intérêt seul qui produit notre amitié* (85). If we take two adjectives and an adverb away from No. 128 we get something simpler, rougher, more direct, thus: *La subtilité est une fausse délicatesse et la délicatesse est une solide subtilité*; just as we feel a loss in vigour and force when *Il n'y a point de libéralité* is replaced by *Ce qu'on nomme libéralité n'est le plus souvent que . . .* (263).

One may perhaps put this point another way by saying that the text of A is closer to the natural expression and to the actual origin of what has been generalized and polished.

A reflection on the violent death of criminals was in A much nearer to a picture of men dying. This is A's version of No. 21: *Ceux qu'on fait mourir affectent quelquefois des constances, des froideurs et des mépris de la mort, pour ne pas penser à elle, de sorte qu'on peut dire que ces froideurs et ces mépris font à leur esprit ce que le bandeau fait à leurs yeux*. Indeed one should note that the process of stylization has begun before A, since the term *bandeau* replaces the more homely *mouchoir* found in the manuscript. The same process is seen at work in No. 57, where the first published version left no doubt that it was a reminiscence of two dominant political figures: *Quoique la grandeur des ministres se flatte de celle de leurs actions elles sont bien souvent les effets du hasard ou de quelque petit dessein.*

In some ways LR is, like his greatest compatriots, a transparent author; he thinks first of a formula close to the reality that he has actually experienced. Only at a second stage does he remove all obvious connections with his own career. We may surmise that the general reflection in No. 254 started in his mind as a picture, which may have been put on paper after his seeing Molière's first staging of *Tartuffe* on 12 May 1664. Here is 254, A version (cf. No. 255, quoted below, p.   ):

L'humilite n'est souvent qu'une feinte soumission que nous employons pour soumettre effectivement tout le monde; c'est un mouvement de l'orgueil par lequel il s'abaisse devant les hommes pour s'élever sur eux; c'est un déguisement et son premeir statagème, mais, quoique ses changements soient presque infinis et qu'il soit admirable sous toutes sortes de figures, il faut avouer néanmoins qu'il n'est jamais si rare ny si extraordinaire que lorsqu'il se cache sous la forme et sous l'habit de l'humilte: car alors on le voit les yeux baissez, dans une contenance modeste et reposée; toutes ses paroles sont douces et respectueuses, pleines d'estime pour les autres et de dédain pour luy-mesme: si on l'en veut croire, il est indigne de tous les honneurs; il ne reçoit les charges où on l'élève que comme un effet de la bonté des hommes et de la faveur aveugle de la fortune. C'est l'orgueil qui joue tous ces personnages que l'on prend pour l'humilité.

The volume we are now studying proves among other things that the cult of the Maxime carried with it a ruthless treatment of ornament, of illustration, of qualification, of all those things which animate and enlarge bare statements. The epigram is a bare statement, and to achieve it all decoration must be sacrificed. LR was clearly not prepared always to go so far, for example in the pages on *amour-propre*, but his efforts have deprived us of vignettes and pictures that his first readers enjoyed. This, for example, in place of what we now read as No. 101: *Il y a de jolies choses que l'esprit ne cherche point, et qu'il trouve toutes achevées en lui-même; il semble qu'elles y soient cachées, comme l'or et les diamants dans le sein de la terre.* Or this, from No. 176: *on trouve sans cesse dans la personne que l'on aime (comme dans une source inépuisable) de nouveaux sujets d'aimer.* . . . . To our taste, the picture of the ever-flowing spring makes the charm of the thought, even more than the brevity for which it had to disappear. Is this the taste of the writer, or of his circle?

We may think that in some cases removal was due to the indelicate nature of the picture evoked rather than to the search for brevity. Here again we are less squeamish, perhaps, and would prefer, to what we read as No. 155, this: *Comme il y a de bonnes viandes qui affadissent le cœur, il y a un mérite fade, et des personnes qui dégoûtent avec des qualités bonnes et estimables.* And even more this, which we should not suspect as being a first version of 239:

Rien ne nous plaît tant que la confiance des grands et des personnes considérables par leurs emplois, par leur esprit ou par leur mérite; elle nous fait sentir un plaisir exquis, et élève merveilleusement notre orgueil, parce que nous le regardons comme un effet de notre fidélité; cependant nous serions remplis de confusion, si nous considérions l'imperfection et la bassesse de sa naissance, car elle vient de la vanité, de l'envie de parler, et de l'impuissance de retenir le secret; de sorte qu'on peut dire que la confiance est comme un relâchement de l'âme, causé par le nombre et par le poids des choses dont elle est pleine.

These cases suggest that LR was ready to sacrifice the image as a dispensable part of any epigram. This is not so. The images which have remained are amazing in their aptness and poetic freshness of suggestion. He uses the sea, nature, minerals, fruit, poison—as will be shown later in this study—with a fitness that only an imaginative writer could command. I cite the abandoned images here to illustrate his technique, not to suggest that he impoverished his own work. His brilliant thought on perspective in judging men and affairs may be thought better or worse without the image that appeared only in A: *Toutes les grandes choses ont leur point de perspective comme les statues.* . . .

The epigram is a metallic form of expression and as one studies it one is apt to think that a thought arose more or less as it appears. But alterations of form are not additional to the thought. Hesitation over formal expression may suggest uncertainty about the thought itself, not merely as to how it should be best expressed. *Ce que l'on conçoit bien s'énonce clairement*, and the converse is also true. It has, indeed, been held against the French classical artists that they only express what is capable of clear expression, and that they miss the most suggestive things, which are not so capable. Since they probably shared Pascal's distrust of imagination, *maîtresse d'erreur et de fausseté*, seeing in it an individual vision of things, hence needing correction by comparison with something more authoritative than any single person could be, it is no wonder that their writing was at the opposite pole from all that could be called romantic.[1]

The variants in A suggest that the thought to which the artist was to give epigrammatic form did not always arise clearly in his mind, and that his task was not, as has been said, one of polishing and chiselling something which was already clear, if clumsy in form. Each will have his own difficulties of interpretation, since epigram is by definition the most cryptic of literary kinds. For my own part I am not at all sure that I understand in any precise sense this reflection: *Tous les sentiments ont chacun un ton de voix, des gestes et des mines qui leur sont propres; ce*

---

[1] On all this Mr. Borgerhoff has suggestive pages in *The Freedom of French Classicism*, 1950.

rapport, bon ou mauvais fait les bons ou mauvais comédiens et c'est ce qui fait aussi que les personnes plaisent ou déplaisent (255). The thought is made a little more obscure by the image of actors, later excised, possibly because it was in itself not clear. Does one understand that the link between feeling and gesture, if well caught, makes a good actor; if ill, a poor actor? If so, the words which remain after 1665, in particular *ce rapport bon ou mauvais*, even with the addition of *agréable ou désagréable*, are not in themselves clear. Do they mean that if the link is unpleasing the person does not please? Or, if the qualities thus linked are unpleasing then the person does not please? Perhaps repeated readings have blunted my sense of something that to a general reader is clear.

Sometimes it is our imperfect knowledge of seventeenth-century language which makes the difficulty. The word 'dégoût' now conveys a positive sense of dislike, as in 131. But the thought of that reflection may have had another meaning, that of ceasing to care for anything, as expressed by the end of A: *une autre (inconstance) qui est plus excusable, qui vient de la fin du goût des choses.*

At times revision brings an actual change in the sense, as in 137, which in A ran as follows: *Nul ne mérite d'être loué de bonté, s'il n'a la force et la hardiesse d'être méchant; toute autre bonté n'est le plus souvent qu'une paresse ou une impuissance de la mauvaise volonté.* One can see why *hardiesse* was removed, but to take out *mauvaise* surely changes the sense from 'absence of evil intent' to 'weakness of will'. The gap is even wider, perhaps, in 246, which both in manuscript and in A has no mention of small interests, but rather emphasizes the intentional exploitation of a show of integrity: here is the A version, shorter than L: *La générosité est un industrieux emploi du désintéressement, pour aller plus tôt à un plus grand intérêt.*

Most of us find it so difficult to be both concise and meaningful that we should be able to appreciate the dilemma of a writer who may glimpse a new thought, may strive to get it clear, and may succeed only in expressing another thought. A poet is led to do this by rhyme and metre. The elaboration of epigram may be a comparable process. The curious thing is that first thoughts are best, sometimes. Things flash into the mind with a perfection that 'art' as a conscious technique could not equal. This I take to be the meaning of No. 101. We know that this did not happen, for instance, in the case of No. 22. The beautiful triptych effect of *maux passés, maux à venir, maux présents* is an effect of art. Even A only achieved an approach: *des maux passés et de ceux qui ne sont pas prêts d'arriver*. In the very next Maxime we may think that first thoughts are best and that LR was not well advised to alter his excellent, dead-pan conclusion: *la plupart des hommes meurent parce qu'on meurt*. A study of 170 is instructive on this point. A reads as follows: *Il n'y a personne qui sache si un procédé net, sincère et honnête est un effet de probité ou d'habileté*. This is more forceful than the present formula *il est difficile de juger*, and when we know that for conventional reasons it was altered from the manuscript reading *Il n'y a que Dieu qui sache . . .*, we can glimpse a first form of great vigour. Curiously enough, the Dutch edition (H) seems to send us back to an even earlier stage: *Il n'y a que Dieu qui sache si un procédé est net, sincère et honnête*. This would seem to me even closer to Biblical passages about the evil heart of man, and as such more searching than any later adaptation.[1]

Not only were first thoughts sometimes best, but we may think that the cult of epigram kept LR's gift of eloquence from its finest flights. One of them we may find in A's version of 247. Beside it the usual text looks colourless and almost trite:

[1] M. Laffond, in *RHLF*, 1966, p. 301, finds this a truism and uses it to suggest that the Dutch text is a later botching of L.

La fidélité est une invention rare de l'amour-propre, par laquelle l'homme, s'érigeant en dépositaire des choses précieuses, se rend lui-même infiniment précieux. De tous les trafics de l'amour-propre c'est celui où il fait le moins d'avances et de plus grands profits; c'est un raffinement de sa politique, avec lequel il engage les hommes par leurs biens, par leur honneur, par leur liberté et par leur vie, qu'ils sont forcés de confier, en quelques occasions, à élever l'homme fidèle au-dessus de tout le monde.

May we not see the same sacrifice of eloquence in the cause of brevity in A's version of 271—*La jeunesse est une ivresse continuelle; c'est la fièvre de la santé, c'est la folie de la raison?* Concision here seems to have resulted in impoverishment (as perhaps in 184, 211, 254). Once again the first edition shows LR to have been faced with the choice between a single brief statement, impressive by the fact that it is alone, and particular impressions that lay behind the single statement. Thus A has as final sentence of 204 this addition: *c'est un attrait fin et délicat et une douceur déguisée.*

Perhaps it is not enough to say that A preserves earlier and longer versions of what we know as epigrams. As we have seen, A preserves the immediate and the particular, which are often absent from epigram. This is why A makes a quite different impression, even on readers of today, from that of the usual text. The pictorial element, not only in actual image, but in concrete word, is not yet fully reduced in 1665. This is to say that at the origin of many epigrams is a pictorial element, an immediacy of impression, a complexity of observation, which is later unified, simplified, arranged. One obvious case of this is No. 249, which in A appears as two separate observations, thus:

Il n'y a pas moins d'éloquence dans le ton de la voix que dans le choix des paroles.

and

Il y a une éloquence dans les yeux et dans l'air de la personne, qui ne persuade pas moins que celle de la parole.

Summing up all these points I would say that A is in itself an admirable tool for the study of LR. His thought is more direct, his expression more individual and more vigorous than in the standard text. The grouping of reflections brings out, more clearly than later separation can do, the main themes on which he reflected. The total impression is also different, less cynical, more analytical, not so much of a warped view as of pitiless clearsightedness in the analysis of a diseased society.

As to the history of the text presented by A, I confess myself thwarted. We need more research before we can reconstruct with any validity how LR made his book. At times he seems to write with a manuscript such as L before him. At times the grouping and phrasing suggest a version very similar to the Dutch edition. This is most obvious in such a case as 14, where the L manuscript reads: *Les Français . . . sont sujets à perdre le souvenir des bienfaits*, and H and A both read *Les hommes sont sujets . . .* ; also 207. When one finds in A, together, 49, 50, 572, 573, all separated in L and all together in H, the same conclusion seems obvious. But in many cases A shows reworkings of reflections found in L and not in H. The whole question needs careful investigation.

As a final point of comparison one may note a theme more constantly recurrent in A than in later versions, and which may well have been a matter of salon discussions: the question of what makes a great man, or more strictly whether we should speak of a hero, as in a novel, meaning a quite different kind of man from the rest. *A une grande vanité près, les héros sont faits comme les autres hommes.* What were known as heroes were people who were *au-dessus de leurs malheurs* (A text of 50), or *dignes d'être en butte à la fortune* (ibid.). Of these people LR had written (L, 129) this: *Ceux qui se sentent du mérite se piquent toujours d'être malheureux pour persuader aux autres et à eux-mêmes qu'ils sont de véritables héros, puisque la mauvaise fortune ne s'opiniâtre jamais à persécuter que les personnes qui ont des qualités extraordinaires.* Heroes (53) are the creation of luck rather than of nature. LR seems to have been attracted by this theme. He suggests that *la gloire des grands hommes* depends on the means they have employed (157), that great actions do not always spring from great designs (160), that 'heroic' can be applied to bad as well as to good qualities (185), that evil men are not to be despised as much as negative (virtueless) men (186). The frequency of this point of view, seen in a context of denial of the classic virtues and of the defeat of the aristocratic ideal in the Fronde, suggests that LR was not making epigrams for mere diversion, but that epigram was his chosen form for the analysis of a declining social type. As M. Bénichou has well said: *Le grandissement héroïque de l'image humaine, la puissance souveraine du moi, la hauteur des désirs sont en cause dans les 'Maximes' beaucoup plus que la bonté (Morales du Grand Siècle, 1948, p. 110).*

4. The Mind behind the *Maximes*

ᛏᐅᏩᛏ

IT is time to investigate the actual content of the all-too-famous little work which appeared in 1665, the year after the first performance of *Tartuffe*. Its main theme was not in fact far removed from the subject of that play; in both the appearance of virtue was belied by the fact. What looks like virtue is not; from this ancient commonplace Molière extracts a dramatic interest, LR proceeds to explore other ingredients. Beneath what passes for piety (12), clemency (15), or constancy (20), he finds temperament, passion, vanity, fear, agitation. What we take for magnanimity may be ambition, for reliability self-interest, for politeness the desire to be well thought of, for generosity the vanity of being thought so. Nearly half the original edition could be described in this way; more reflections suggest this contrast than anything else. Appearance and reality: in a final page on the attitude to death the author admits that his theme has been just this: *après avoir parlé de tant de vertus apparentes il est raisonnable de dire quelque chose de la fausseté du mépris de la mort* (504).

It is thus not surprising that such reflections should be received as a manual of cynicism and their author taken to be a disillusioned pessimist. The choice language and the brevity enforced the impression: *On ne loue que pour être loué*. Could the expression of vanity and self-interest be more pointed? Need one look further for the message of the book than this obvious debunking of those qualities we profess to admire in other people: magnanimity, pity, bravery, generosity, sincerity? As if to make the attitude quite clear, the volume opened with a two-page diatribe on self-interest, in all behaviour, in everyone, especially piquant in cases (such as professions of piety) where the language would suggest the opposite.

So far as it went this was not a false impression. We do not know enough of LR's character to say if he was or was not a cynic at heart, but it is clear that he wrote like one. And not only in 1665. He removed some of the more shocking reflections, but later editions were not inspired by any attitude noticeably more optimistic. And his life seemed to fit this attitude; a disillusioned and disappointed Frondeur, he had seen the worst in men and his offence seemed to be that he put down what he had seen without palliating or extenuating. His adversary and counterpart Retz, as was to appear from his *Mémoires*, shared his view, but there was all the difference between cold epigrams and a long confession of sins and errors. Some opinions have survived, written by friends who were allowed to see the manuscript before publication. These leave no room for doubt that they were shocked. Mme de La Fayette wrote: *Quelle corruption il faut avoir dans l'esprit et dans le cœur pour être capable d'imaginer tout cela* (Éd. Pléiade, p. 690). Virtue as usually thought of disappears in this book, said another, Mme de Schomberg: *Après la lecture de cet écrit on demeure persuadé qu'il n'y a ni vice ni vertu à rien et que l'on fait nécessairement toutes les actions de la vie.* Another remarked that the book *découvrait les parties honteuses de la vie civile et de la société humaine, sur lesquelles il fallait tirer le rideau* (ibid., 691, 694).

It is necessary for us to realize this sense of shock and scandal evoked by the first appearance of the *Maximes*. Necessary, but difficult, for we must remember that the mind, as modern science has revealed it, was a sealed book in the seventeenth century. The science of psychology, the subconscious, all that is for us evoked by the name of Freud, must be banished if we are to enter the world of 1660. LR did not, of course, discover sins and vices and the 'evil heart of man'. What he revealed would not have been unknown to the Hebrew prophets, or to the Greek dramatists, or to Shakespeare. His originality, as we shall see, was not in the revelation but in the explanation of behaviour. About sin as such, man's ingratitude, vanity, double-tongued evasions, about these things he knew no more than any *directeur de conscience* of his own day. In his isolation of self-interest he strikes us as less profound than Bossuet and Pascal. He is interesting not in his exposure but in his analysis, and this is clearer to us than it could be to the public of 1665. His manuscripts and his additions to his work up to the end of his life make it clear that an attack on what was called 'virtue' was only one of his objectives, and one that was possibly put forward to create a sensation, as it in fact did.

These epigrams, in fact, speak less of false virtue than of mixed virtue. His constant suggestion is not that virtue is not present, but that it is only one of the factors present. To speak of generosity is not so much out of place as over-simple. There are many factors in what we dismiss as a single quality. Our names for the virtues are in fact umbrella-words. We think we are describing one thing, but what we speak of is in fact an amalgam. Nobody has put this point better than André Gide: *Croire à des sentiments simples est une façon simple de considérer les sentiments*. One example from many will suffice for the moment. Harking back to his experiences of civil war LR reflects on cases where military commanders have restrained their troops from plunder or massacre or blockade. Retz tells us that Condé's army could deny supplies of bread to Paris and thus exercise a stranglehold over the capital. No wonder that much was made of a commander who showed the virtue of 'clemency'.

But let us read No. 16: *Cette clémence, dont on fait une vertu, se pratique tantôt par vanité, quelquefois par paresse, souvent par crainte, et presque toujours par tous les trois ensemble.* In the same way another reflection suggests no less than five motives for bravery in battle (213). To speak of bravery at all is to give a single name to what may be an infinite number of gradations: *La parfaite valeur et la poltronnerie complète sont deux extrémités où l'on arrive rarement. L'espace qui est entre-deux est vaste . . .* (215).

Many people seem to read LR as if he were saying that what we call a virtue is only . . . self-interest. But this is not what he says. He probes motives and finds variety where we see or speak of a single quality. Further than this he hesitates to go. The *Maximes* are full of uncertainty. He suggests that we can assume the presence of several motives but we cannot say, in any given case, which was decisive, dominant; *il est difficile . . .* is a frequent formula. Life and behaviour are beyond our analysis. Only God knows the heart: *Il n'y a que Dieu qui sache si un procédé, net, sincère et honnête, est plutôt un effet de probité que d'habileté.* Since mention of God had to be cut out from the published Maxime, it is the more important for us to realize that LR's thought was in line with the Bible and the Fathers of the Church.

To think of the *Maximes* as putting on all our acts the ticket, so to speak, of self-interest is therefore to do violence to one of their main features, LR's respect for the mystery of motive. Motive can be suggested but never confidently affirmed. This line of thought is brilliantly expressed in a Maxime which has been called the key to all the rest (436): *Il est plus aisé de connaître l'homme en général que de connaître un homme en particulier.* This suggests that the French classical writers have been misunderstood. We think of them as writing about man in general because they had mastered personal knowledge and were thus able to speak with confidence of all men. With LR, one of the

most clear-sighted of them, almost the reverse is the case:
there is no claim to know the individual. All we can do
after intense scrutiny of behaviour is to say that many
factors may be present, and that one which seems always
present is self-preservation. In what measure a particular
case shows the various ingredients of behaviour, this we
can never know. We must remain in the dark and realize
that our statements are approximations, since our instruments are too insensitive to register actual motives. We find
LR thinking on these lines in a reflection later reduced
and made impenetrable (106, H 145):

> On ne saurait compter toutes les espèces de vanité: pour cela
> il faut savoir le détail des choses, et comme il est presque
> infini, de là vient que si peu de gens sont savants et que nos
> connaissances sont superficielles[1] et imparfaites. On décrit les
> choses au lieu de les définir. En effet on ne les connaît et on ne
> peut les connaître qu'en gros, et par des marques communes.
> C'est comme si quelqu'un disait que le corps humain est droit
> et composé de différentes parties, sans dire la matière, la
> situation, les fonctions, les rapports et les différences des ses
> parties.

This sense of mystery before an organism whose complexity we can hardly begin to understand is perhaps the
most original part of his work. Properly read, every sentence of the famous opening reflection of 1665 on self-
love refers to mystery, to qualities which we sense but
cannot see. These pages are an attempt to describe the
indescribable, to suggest the impenetrable. For example:

> De cette nuit qui le couvre naissent les ridicules persuasions
> qu'il a de lui-même; de là viennent ses erreurs, ses ignorances,
> ses grossièretés et ses niaiseries sur son sujet; de là vient
> qu'il croit que ses sentiments sont morts lorsqu'ils ne sont
> qu'endormis, qu'il s'imagine n'avoir plus envie de courir dès
> qu'il se repose et qu'il pense avoir perdu tous les goûts qu'il a

---

[1] H has here *superflues*, which I take to be a printer's error.

nassasiés. Mais cette obscurité épaisse qui le cache à lui-même n'empêche pas qu'il ne voit parfaitement ce qui est hors de lui; en quoi il est semblable à nos yeux, qui découvrent tout et sont aveugles seulement pour eux-mêmes. En effet, dans ses plus grands intérêts et dans ses plus importantes affaires, où la violence de ses souhaits appelle toute son attention, il voit, il sent, il entend, il imagine, il soupçonne, il pénètre, il devine tout, de sorte qu'on est tenté de croire que chacune de ses passions a une magie qui lui est propre.

Surely this is writing of a high order. Lucid in form, short unremarkable phrases, few images, most of the stress on the single verb—these features are not usually combined with the description of something that no human eye has seen or brain registered. Apparently the only way of describing the quality called *amour-propre* is to make it personal. The phrases are understandable as applied to a human being; perhaps even more to an animal, in a lair, taking precautions against surprise, running, resting, feeding, hiding, finding no rest. We are not, as we thought, in the domain of critical assessment, still less in the domain of phrase-making, we are reading about magic, a picture is conjured up before our eyes; we watch the imagination at work. What it shows is a monster, something unnatural. The mood of scorn, discernible in many epigrams, is absent. The attitude is one of respect, almost awe, before something ubiquitous and mysterious. Yet we know what is being described: the power and plight of fallen man is here more imposing and impressive than in a Bossuet sermon. This is an Augustinian passage.

Such writing is so far from polite letters as then understood, from what Sercy was offering to his readers in his *Recueils*, that we can see why LR withdrew it, annoyed perhaps that it should be dismissed as 'galimatias'. It may be significant also that he refused to cut it up into Maximes, sensing it as a unity. It has the unity of a poem, classical in penetration but with a plastic power which we are not accustomed to regard as classical.

If we look for it we can see in and behind the Maximes which at first sight appear cynical something of this same painful penetration into mystery, this encounter with dark powers which lame man's choice and decision. Such a power is mood, *l'humeur*, a state of mind for which we cannot account and which we cannot command. This emerges in LR's memoirs. The Frondeur had known occasions when the opportunity was not seized, when power was not used and the challenge of an occasion was not met, or was met by one party and not the other. No less than eleven Maximes are concerned with this. Another such dark power is indolence (*paresse*). Again we have a whole group, of which one was withdrawn after the first edition, surely because it was so outspoken (630, A 290):

De toutes les passions celle qui est la plus inconnue à nous-mêmes c'est la paresse; elle est la plus ardente et la plus maligne de toutes, quoique sa violence soit insensible et que les dommages qu'elle cause soient très cachés. Si nous considérons attentivement son pouvoir nous verrons qu'elle se rend en toutes rencontres maîtresse de nos sentiments, de nos intérêts et de nos plaisirs; c'est la rémore qui a la force d'arrêter les plus grands vaisseaux; c'est une bonace plus dangereuse aux plus importantes affaires que les écueils et que les plus grandes tempêtes. Le repos de la paresse est un charme secret de l'âme qui suspend soudainement les plus ardentes poursuites et les plus opiniâtres résolutions. Pour donner enfin la véritable idée de cette passion, il faut dire que la paresse est comme une béatitude de l'âme, qui la console de toutes ses pertes, et qui lui tient lieu de tous les biens.

Analysis as subtle as this could not possibly be the result of tea-party conversations. Every line, every clause, suggests long and patient observation, and not at all the bias usually attributed to LR, but rather an absence of

bias, a coolness of approach, almost clinical in its desire
to resist current concepts and to watch passions and
moods actually at work. LR is given no credit for what
perhaps made up the chief novelty of his writing, this
objectivity of attitude, patience in distinguishing small
hidden features of behaviour, untrammelled persistence
in seeing how things actually work, how men really
behave. As he continued, no doubt the quality of bias,
of *prévention*, became more marked: he seemed content
to find evidence of what his own misfortunes had taught
him to suspect. But no writer of his time seems to have
possessed his gift for discarding assumptions and fashions
and looking at behaviour with fresh eyes.

Another dark power which he revealed was the physical
framework of all conduct. We do . . . what our bodies
and our physical humours allow us to do. The effect of
temperament, for instance, is usually noted in cases where
it breaks out, in anger or violent action. Was LR not the
first to call attention to the constant unseen influence of
physical constitution upon behaviour? This early reflection was later split up for the purpose of a Maxime:

> Nous nous apercevons des emportements et des mouvements
> extraordinaires de nos humeurs et de notre tempérament
> comme de la violence de la colère. Mais personne quasi ne
> s'aperçoit que ces humeurs ont un cours ordinaire et réglé,
> qui meut et tourne doucement notre volonté à des actions
> différentes. Elles roulent ensemble (s'il faut ainsi dire) et exer-
> cent successivement leur empire, de sorte qu'elles ont une part
> considérable à toutes nos actions, dont nous croyons être les
> seuls auteurs, et le caprice de l'humeur est encore plus bizarre
> que celui de la fortune. (H 136.)

We may not agree with the fruits of this talent for observation, but we must not miss its originality. In a day when
psychology in our sense was unknown, a talent which
could discover beneath conscious behaviour laws and
mechanisms working unseen had at least something new

to say. Nothing was likely to surprise a man who had discovered that we are far from knowing what we really want (295).

Nor was he satisfied to discern dark powers only within man. Those outside him are no less formidable and give a new depth to the analysis. These are referred to in several ways, which we might sum up under the single word 'chance'. Were it not for chance, our qualities, good and bad, might never be seen: *La fortune fait paraître nos vertus et nos vices, comme la lumière fait paraître les objets* (380). One thinks of Flaubert's remark: *Il y a en moi un tas de vices qui n'ont jamais mis le nez à la fenêtre.* LR is more cautious, and suggests a wider range of conduct: *Toutes nos qualités sont incertaines et douteuses, en bien comme en mal, et elles sont presque toutes à la merci des occasions* (470). It seems as though LR had learned from Montaigne of the gap between intention and fact. We give praise to prudence, or the faculty of taking thought, but the outcome of any affair may be unaffected by such thought as we take (65). Yet prudence is called our sole defence: it fuses good and bad qualities into a shield against life's attack (182).

So the content of the *Maximes* would seem to be very inadequately described as cynical reaction to misfortune. It turns out to be an extensive and original assessment of the factors of experience, which gives particular attention to vital forces and shows small respect for what are called the Stoic virtues. Such a thing as reason, for example, which in Descartes could dominate the passions, emerges in this assessment as captive, limited, deceived. The mind is at the mercy of the heart, and indeed the body. The fact is that we are not strong enough to follow our reason, to go by reason (42, 43).

The friend who wrote an introductory essay to the first edition of the *Maximes* used the happy simile of the beleaguered city to describe the heart of man as he appears in these epigrams, attacked from all sides and able to offer only limited or spasmodic resistance:

> . . . il regarde le cœur de l'homme corrompu, attaqué de l'orgueil et de l'amour-propre et environné de mauvais exemples, comme le commandant d'une ville assiégée à qui l'argent a manqué; il fait de la monnaie du cuir et du carton; cette monnaie a la figure de la bonne, on la débite pour le même prix, mais ce n'est que la misère et le besoin qui lui donnent cours parmi le assiégés. (Éd. Pléiade, p. 393.)

This would suggest that LR had been led to reflect on *amour-propre*, not as a cynical explanation of the human predicament, but as that obscure instinct of self-preservation which he came to see as involved in all the acts of the creature called man. He seems to have sensed in this force something more biological than ethical, something more like instinct than conscious design, the instinct to keep going, to keep one's head above water, *sauve qui peut*, defence rather than attack. Action is thus seen as reaction, a reply to demands made by society and by other people, and an attitude of defence common to all men, not confined to certain classes or temperaments: *Il est dans tous les états de la vie et dans toutes les conditions; il vit partout et il vit de tout* (563).

Is this a true view? The answers given to this question have varied according to the experience from which they are made. Sainte-Beuve said that we find LR grow more true as we grow older. Most of us tend to ask the question too soon. It is not, as one would think from many books, the question to start with, perhaps not the important question. Let us find out, if we can, what LR was talking about before we ask whether he was right. We have seen that it takes into account qualities and forces not thought very important by stoics and rationalists, that it seems to give more attention to capacities and existential attitudes than to moral principles. The picture, as one might expect if one recalled LR's public life, is unheroic, often pessimist in suggestion. But none can miss its vivid insights into the realities of social life. Seventeenth-century man emerges more vividly from these metallic comments on his activity than from most histories.

Trying to do justice to all the features we have reviewed, let us see what sort of picture is presented. It is a picture of man as more weak than vicious. On the evil heart of man it is indeed as clear as the Bible or the Christian Fathers. *La malignité de notre nature* is not questioned. Man has no power over events. He is at the mercy of fortune, and so insecure that his moral statements (such as promises) are meaningless (38). He lacks the power to be reasonable, or to master his passions and his moods. He is beset at all points by fear and ignorance. Fear indeed is a recurrent theme in the *Maximes*, fear of other people (16, 18), fear of death (21), fear of injustice (78), fear of shame (213), fear of battle (215), fear in the midst of hope (515). The only resource is to hang on, to maintain his position by any and every means. A phrase excised from an early reflection is *la violente passion de se conserver*. Such a being, a target in a hostile world, cannot afford the luxury of high principles, still less of true virtue. He has not the strength to tell the truth (641). His only defence is pride and the fact that he does not know his weakness (36). He has no time, in more than one sense, for anything outside himself: his vanity is protean (506).

It is a gloomy picture, not very different from that of Pascal. Here too is portrayed *la misère de l'homme*, lacking the piercing Pascalian insights into human inability to know the why and wherefore of our condition, but more modern, more scientific in its insistence on and analysis of self-preservation. Both are pessimists, both wrote from an Augustinian standpoint, both (has this been noticed?) see *grandeur* as well as *misère*. LR knows and refers with respect to the Christian virtues, humility, charity, sincerity.

He goes so far as to say that man's intellectual power is greater than has yet appeared (482). He admires the fact that we possess capacities of which we are not aware until they emerge. He is not even wholly gloomy about the role of chance in our lives: chance may bring out our best qualities (345, 404).

This inquiry into behaviour may not be reducible to a system, but it has certain distinguishing marks. Perhaps these might be re-stated in summary form. From among the points already mentioned I would say that three in particular combine to allow him to analyse conduct at a deeper level than is often supposed.

He is sensitive to physical forces in human behaviour. He has at the same time respect for quite different forces, which seem external to man altogether. He renews the ancient distinction between essence and existence. Some not unfair picture of his thought may emerge if we consider each of these separately.

Mme de Schomberg seems to have been near the mark when she said that the *Maximes* persuaded her that all human action is mechanical and determined. At least fifteen in the standard text suggest this. They suggest that the passions are out of our control: *la durée de nos passions ne dépend pas plus de nous que la durée de notre vie* (5). We are not free either to love or to stop loving: why then complain of infidelity or philandering (577)? Our resistance to the passions is due to their weakness more than to our strength (122). We deceive ourselves in imagining that we give up vices: it is they who leave us (192). Love is compared to a fever: we can alter neither its force nor its duration (638). It is as easy to fall in love as to fall ill (183). As with fever, what we take for abatement of love may be temporary, or a change of emotion (193). Even apart from strong emotions, the mind seems dependent on the body; an early version of No. 44 suggests that LR was reflecting on failure or lack of intellectual power, and that he saw in this a case of failure of nerve, in an almost literal sense (H 20): *La faiblesse de l'esprit est mal nommée; c'est en effet la faiblesse du tempéra-ment, qui n'est autre chose qu'une impuissance d'agir, et un manque de principe de vie.* We need to know a good deal about seventeenth-century medical theory to see what is meant here. LR (and even Descartes?) seems to have thought of health as dependent on some physical 'life-force' which defied definition. The hesitation between *'tempérament'* and *'cœur'* is a sign of probing uncertainty. One kind of anger is said to have a physical cause, if I interpret *ardeur de complexion* aright (601). LR defines gravity as a physical mystery adopted to cover lack of intelligence (257). Montaigne had said much the same thing in *L'Art de conférer.*

The history of No. 297 would be interesting to know in this regard. It seems likely that it was attached to 45, and it suggests an attempt to find a scientific basis for apparent whimsicality of mood. What is probably the oldest text has been quoted above. It enforces our inability to alter our constitution, moral no less than physical. So I read No. 189: *Il semble que la nature ait prescrit à chaque homme dès sa naissance des bornes pour les vertus et pour les vices.* This led LR the artist to one of his most successful images. Vices he likens to innkeepers who await us on life's journey. Were we to travel the same road again, we should find ourselves lodging in the same inns (191; cf. L 218). Again the thought may have been sharpened by close reading of Montaigne.

What we should make of this line of thought is not at first clear. It occurs in Pascal, and may have been shared by Descartes. La Bruyère seems to adopt it in places, but I think as a literary artifice only: his sketch of Champagne, unable while digesting his plentiful dinner to imagine that people anywhere can be dying of hunger, is brilliant, and artificial by comparison. LR conveys something of a scientific attitude, in his patient probing of awkward cases.

We have seen that the artist who imagined morals as affected by physique is also the artist who discerns forces outside ourselves which may control behaviour. His respect for chance is unique, as far as I know, in the French classical writers. Texts in epigrammatic form are of course designed to conceal their origins, and only rarely can we conjecture the history of a Maxime. All the same, the formulas are surprising. Our stock of wisdom may vanish, like our material possessions: *Notre sagesse n'est pas moins à la merci de la fortune que nos biens.* (The editors of Pléiade/2 see this as a possible echo of Cicero.) It is not wise to disregard fortune since it has part in acts which we think of as due to our own merit. The thought appears in two forms and it would seem that LR was concerned to make more explicit what had appeared in his first edition:

De plusieurs actions différentes que la fortune arrange comme il lui plaît, il s'en fait plusieurs vertus (631).

Ce que nous prenons pour des vertus n'est souvent qu'un assemblage de diverses actions et de divers intérêts que la fortune ou notre industrie savent arranger . . . (1).

Charron (and possibly Italian writers) had made the circle in which LR moved reluctant to confuse actions and qualities (a good action need not mean a good man). The fact of chastity does not argue that a woman is chaste. Chance brings out our qualities, thereby both surprising us and suggesting that we may have qualities which are never tested in fact. We shall see later that he calls men great who have had the luck to prove great qualities, which others may possess but have had no opportunity to exhibit with success. Preferment, for instance, may be a result of our luck rather than of our merit: *La fortune se sert quelquefois de nos défauts pour nous élever* (403). Sudden preferment is a challenge we may not be able to sustain (449). Both LR and La Bruyère were tempted to compare the fate of those who deserved promotion and got it, with that of those who did not, and also got it (449; cf. Éd. Pléiade, p. 795). We complain of fortune when it is unkind to us, but the moralist is more interested by the opposite, for instance No. 57: Fortune may be our friend. It may ensure our good behaviour (154). It brings to light qualities which are otherwise hidden (344). It brings out qualities both bad and good (380). Our qualities are at the mercy of fortune (470), but this is a means of self-knowledge (345). These thoughts are expressed by the artist, not in any dry or dogmatic way, but using images perfectly chosen. That qualities emerge by accident, was no great discovery. It needs an artist to see and express this fact by suggesting a darkened room, in which we see nothing until light comes and shows us what was there all the time.

On what one may call the 'run of luck' one can imagine the salon discussions, reflected perhaps in No. 60: *La fortune tourne tout à l'avantage de ceux qu'elle aime*; or in No. 309: *Il y a des gens qui semblent destinés à être sots*. A run of luck seems to have been called one's 'star' (58, 165). Some people turn even ill luck to their profit (59), so that wisdom would lie in reckoning carefully with chance, and in letting no occasion escape unheeded (343, 392). Yet even prudence is not the last word; prudence may be without effect (65). At times, daring or risk may serve us better, even folly (310). In any case we can never guarantee our behaviour, since we never know what chance may bring (574).

Fortune being incalculable, all that is in our power is the way we take it. Several Maximes couple chance and mood. Our happiness depends on the one no less than on the other. This line of thought, evident in Nos. 17,

47, and others, achieved its finest form in 435. In four operative words a view of affairs is expressed which challenges all normal attitudes of education and morality: *La fortune et l'humeur gouvernent le monde.* Our reaction is, of course, shock, surprise, denial. What about planning, training, government, monarchy, nobility? So, as often, the epigram opens up a world of discussion. What has been called '*l'éducation politique de Louis XIV*' has aroused controversy, and we must remember that LR witnessed this education of a prince at close quarters. Perhaps it was with the King's youth in mind that he suggested that luck and mood are in the last analysis the things that count.

Let us see how LR renews the ancient distinction between essence and existence. It may be that in the sophisticated circle around him he missed this element, which Montaigne had stressed (and before him, of course, the greater Schoolmen) of the gap between thinking and being. Awareness of this gap comes out frequently in the *Maximes.* There is all the difference between imagining a situation and being in that situation. It is easy to show sympathy, when one is not affected (19). Advice is easy; conduct is of another order: *On donne des conseils, mais on n'inspire point de conduite* (378). We find an even sharper expression of the same thought: *Les vieillards aiment à donner de bons préceptes, pour se consoler de n'être plus en état de donner de mauvais exemples* (93). 'What man by taking thought can add a cubit to his stature?' Maxime 65 seems to me not far removed from the Gospel: ... *la prudence ne saurait nous assurer d'aucun événement.* There is all the difference between the desire to be brave ... and bravery (616), between friendship and friends (427), between qualities and their practice (437). Mme de Sablé may have had a hand in this discussion, as she prints a similar formulation even more pungent: *Il n'y a point de vraies grandes qualités, si on ne les met en usage.* The man with heroic qualities cannot be a 'hero' unless his qualities have been tested in battle (53, 153).

Thoughts like these suggest that LR would have enjoyed Molière's comic variations on this same gap between notion and fact, Sosie's insistence that *la chose est incompréhensible mais cela ne laisse pas d'être*, or the servant's pleasure in stating that, in defiance of all the rules of medicine, *le cocher est mort*.

5. Influence of the Salon

Is it possible to narrow any further our answer to the question as to what the *Maximes* are really about? Analysis of conduct may cover a wide field. All depends on what spheres of life are brought into consideration. The *Maximes* are known to be what is called salon literature. Yet they clearly go beyond the conversation that could be heard in any salon. In some cases they echo memories of civil war. They search for motive; they explore the forces which affect conduct. But in a specific sense, what sort of conduct?

Our evidence as to what was discussed in the salons is incomplete. Like the novels and letters of that age, conversation seems to have centred on qualities, their display, their definition. Noël Vallant, Mme de Sablé's doctor and scribe, was fortunately an industrious man, and thanks to his detailed evidence (and to its presentation by M. Ivanov) we can form a picture of what went on in the salons which saw the formulation of the first Maximes.

Madeleine de Souvray, Marquise de Sablé, was a woman in whom experience and temperament combined, as in the similar case of Catherine de Vivonne, to make the ideal hostess. Married in 1614, her first child born in 1618, she appears in *Le Grand Cyrus* as Parthénice. Her career links the stormy days of Richelieu and the adventures of the Fronde to the placidity of an elegant social group, meeting in her Paris *hôtel*. So the talk in her salon may have had overtones, as her guests had certainly memories, of the social upheaval, the conspiracy, and the double-dealing which the Fronde had produced. Mme de Sablé had been courted by Montmorency, who was executed in 1632 for conspiracy. She was constantly in debt; she says in a letter of 1664 that her income of 80,000 écus had never allowed her to buy the lace from Genoa that she would have liked to put on her dresses. She was in touch with many milieux: one of her sons was a bishop; another was killed in action at Dunkirk. She was engaged in constant discussions with Jansenists. Ivanov quotes a letter of 1644 in which Mazarin comments, with some apprehension apparently, on the freedom of discussion between such great persons as the Duc d'Enghien, Arnaud d'Andilly, the Princesse de Guémené, and the Duchesse de Nemours, all under Mme de Sablé's roof: *si parla di tutti liberamente*. Tallemant says that no court intrigue left her uninterested and that her liking for cabals was notorious, suggesting that this drew her to the Jansenists. Her reading was wide; d'Andilly sent her his translation of Josephus. She knew her Montaigne. To compare Théophile (de Viau) with Voiture seemed to her an outrage. Some elements have been preserved of a discussion on the Spanish character: she thought Spaniards much overrated, not really polite despite their reputation, and in literature past their peak. When Pascal visited her she taxed him with being unfair to the Jesuits. Mme de Sablé was not only a person of charm, but an excellent cook, so much so that in 1668 the Queen, Monsieur, and Madame actually dined at her house. Kind-hearted, keen on discussion, more attracted to morals than to history, she introduced into her salon the habit of serious argument, and appointed a secretary to take notes.

This is the true context of the *Maximes*. They were born in a milieu which we have perhaps too easily thought of as merely social, as concerned with the trivialities of tea-table conversation. We may correct this impression by noting some of the epigrams which were excluded from LR's second edition, presumably because they went too near the bone, and recalled too vividly a reality which people were anxious to forget. LR's thoughts would not have been, perhaps, the gems they are had it not been for the encouragement and the criticism of both the hostess and the guests of the salon. As he wrote to her: *vous savez bien . . . que les sentences ne sont sentences qu'après que vous les avez approuvées.*

With this background in mind we are liable to be disappointed to find that so little of the discussion which undoubtedly went on appears in the *Maximes* themselves. Of the discussions on Calvinism, on history, on national character, on death, on stoicism, of all these there is hardly a trace. The two Maximes on death tell us nothing of what form the discussion may have taken. We must conclude that LR has either not retained or that he has found unusable most of the views to which he must have listened. Possibly he felt that as an aristocrat, *qui n'avait pas étudié*, his own views were not important.

His reflections leave us in no doubt, however, that the talk turned constantly on definitions of character and of 'good qualities', what the *Maximes* call '*les vertus*'. These were obligatory elements of polite conversation. Politeness, flattery, complaisance, all the things Alceste objected to, these were attractive subjects to put on the *tapis*, and to discuss, with an air of scepticism, in order to determine how much, or how little, was meant by the obligatory formulas of good breeding. One member of the circle, Arnaud d'Andilly, was known apparently as liking to pose as expert in matters of friendship: *il faisait le professeur en amitié.* Where all seem to have joined in is in matters of form, that is the exact formulation of what might be said or sustained. We must not think of the *Maximes* as pedantic formulations of what their author felt to be 'the Truth'. The tone of salon discussion probably tended rather to cruising around an idea and to concentric suggestions of approach. Both in form and in content the discussion was probably artificial to a degree which to us of a later age might seem unreal. It might well have made upon us much the same impression as the volumes of polite verse issued by that astute bookseller Charles Sercy. It was in fact in one of these that the famous pages on *amour-propre* were first printed. One has only to peruse the surrounding items to experience the jar, the shock, of having moved from a world of imagination and powerful writing, and astonishing concepts, back into a small world of convention and pastime and affectation. The explanation, no doubt, is that the games of a salon were the cradle, so to say, of epigrams which, when once put before a large public, were read by all the world.

There is no evidence that LR thought meanly of the salon microcosm in which he was compelled to move. He can be withering in his exposure of human vices, but he never wrote scornfully of the discussions which he watched and guided. They were, of course, too valuable for him to risk losing them, and it is likely that he felt himself a part of that little world, as he had once done of the world of the aristocratic conspirators who formed the group called '*les Importants*'.

It is not, I think, impossible to discern from the *Maximes* both the frequent subjects of salon discussion and LR's own angle on them. Behaviour, intelligence, sincerity, feelings, qualities of heart and mind, all these would naturally be on the agenda, not by any special desire on the part of the hostess, but because these were things of which everyone present in such a '*cercle*' was bound to have had some experience. The salons discovered, and presented to great writers like Pascal and Molière and LR, a new subject-matter, or rather a subject-matter which had so far been embedded in novels and manuals of 'civility'.

This new subject-matter may, I think, be defined as the reactions of ordinary people to the process of social existence. We may surmise what it was by excluding what it was not. It was clearly not business conversation, nor military, nor political, nor religious. All such subjects were barred, either because they were dangerous, or because they would interest and affect only a small proportion of those who took part. Mme de Rambouillet and her successors, among whom Mme de Sablé may be counted perhaps the most distinguished, sought a subject of general interest, common to the mixed gathering. That subject could only be what people of different professions and social rank have in common, that is reflection, reaction, to manners, to social habits, to any matters of 'universal' concern. What in fact the textbooks of literature are accustomed to refer to as one of the attributes of French classicism, its interest in the human, the general, the universal, may here be watched in process of growth. It arises, not according to any theory, nor at the behest of any lawgiver or pedant, but almost by elimination, as it were. Given the French social instinct and the French love of conversation, given the fact of a dispossessed leisure class, barred from politics and government and disdaining commerce, what is there left to talk about except to comment, in a general, human, or abstract way, on people, what they do, how they look, what reactions they provoke? And what is this but the classic (rather than classical) French exercise of the critical intelligence?

This makes Mme de Rambouillet and her imitators effective, even if unconscious, disciples of Montaigne. It is his views that are moulded by successive salons. It is his universality which in the salon found a social framework and field of action. For it was Montaigne who had said that you did not need to be great or famous to experience all the problems of the moral life: *On attache tout aussi bien toute la philosophie morale à une vie populaire et privée qu'à une vie de plus riche étoffe. Chaque homme porte la forme entière de l'humaine condition.* It was Montaigne, we recall, who wrote that discussion of conversation which Pascal called incomparable, and who in the course of it had drawn up the rules of polite conversation. His rules correspond closely to the habits of such salons as we are now considering. Why they did so has not been submitted to scientific investigation: probably not so much because they actually copied him as because he unconsciously foreshadowed them. Here, as in so many things, he appears as a great architect of French classicism.

Montaigne had defined a social group in which the essential activity was the polite, but so far as possible natural, expression of different points of view:

> Le plus fructueux et naturel exercice de notre esprit, c'est à mon gré la conférence . . . L'étude des livres, c'est un mouvement languissant et faible qui n'échauffe point, là où la conférence apprend et exerce en un coup . . . J'entre en conférence et en dispute avec grande liberté et facilité . . . nulles propositions m'étonnent, nulle créance me blesse, quelque contrariété qu'elle aie à la mienne . . . les contradictions des jugements ne m'offensent ni m'altèrent; elles m'éveillent seulement et m'exercent . . . Quand on me contrarie, on éveille mon attention, non pas ma colère; je m'avance vers celui qui me contredit, qui m'avertit: la cause de la vérité devrait être la cause commune de l'un et de l'autre. (III. 8.)

From such discussion Montaigne would exclude what we might call unnatural argument, such as things said from memory or culled from a book, and thus all professional language and conversation; everyone must make himself generally intelligible; none must take charge, monopolize the talk. He seems to have had confidence in the general sense of the meeting, not only to keep the discussion on right lines, but to advance it with profit, to prevent its getting sanded up in matters uninteresting to those who were taking part. *Ce n'est pas tant la force et la subtilité que je demande comme l'ordre, l'ordre qui se voit tous les jours aux altercations des bergers et des enfants de boutique, jamais entre nous . . . leur propos suit son cours. . . .* Of course, in 1583 Montaigne may have had very different discussions in mind from those which actually took place in Paris in the sixties of the next century. He would probably have thought these too artificial and superficial, too inhibited with regard to the great subjects of human argument to have been really profitable. But it is astonishing to see how closely in many ways 'salon talk' is what he had in mind, astonishing chiefly because we have thought of him as an individualist boxed up in his own time, not as an author whom LR and Pascal and their generation would know, read, and enjoy.

It would be easy to show how the epigrams of LR, of Esprit, and of Mme de Sablé herself are natural points or angles in a discussion, and even more often express the extreme points of that discussion. *La plupart des amis dégoûtent de l'amitié*: the very phrase allows us to imagine views expressed about friends and friendship, about the quality as found in actual people, views which may well have ranged widely in opposing directions. Some may have enforced the ideal quality we call friendship, as superior to glimpses of the quality which this or that person we count as friend may allow us to have. Others may have resisted this platonism, and questioned the existence of friendship distinct from what we see in our friends. In this case someone does seem to have said at some point: what about religion? Is piety just what you happen to find in a pious person? Or is there something more, a quality, a quintessence? Probably not on the spot, but after further discussion, reflection, interchange of notes, LR might then produce a pleasing formula, balanced, yet sardonic, suggesting by its oppositions what may have been implicit in the talk, but as paradox, which required a master of speech to give it perfect expression. *La plupart des amis dégoûtent de l'amitié et la plupart des dévots dégoûtent de la dévotion* (427).

How then are we to understand such thoughts? As tenets of a corpus of doctrine, as subtle and snide examples of a cynical mind? As playful expressions of what might be maintained? As pointers to a truth which may be unpleasant but which leads to a larger view of the human scene? Almost by definition there is no way of proving which interpretation was true, is true, may be true. Epigram is anonymous and impenetrable; personal conviction which may have gone to its making is lost in the metallic opaque suggestion of a few chosen words. It allows its maker to hide within it and never be seen. Hence its mystery, and hence the error of those who have seen in these epigrams the personal echo of a disappointed man. They are that, perhaps, but much more than that.

We could surely not go wrong in thinking of love as a constant subject of discussion. After all, most novels and plays treated the subject, then as now, and it would have special attraction for a society still *précieux* in spirit, that is anxious to avoid what might be thought vulgar and base, and to think and speak of what is refined, intellectual, distinguished. If my memory serves, physical love is referred to only once in the *Maximes* and then in terms which seem to me nearly *précieux*. This is in No. 68, which has every sign of preserving, as a fossil in the stone, echoes of many discussions. I quote the first printed form, from A : *Il est malaisé de définir l'amour: tout ce qu'on en peut dire est que dans l'âme c'est une passion de régner; dans les esprits, c'est une sympathie; et dans le corps, ce n'est qu'une envie cachée et délicate de jouir de ce qu'on aime après beaucoup de mystères.*

We may assume that Maximes excluded after LR's first edition and later printed by one of his friends were so excluded because they had been too quickly incorporated into LR's own work, since they belonged to others in the group as much as to him. Thus: *L'amour est à l'âme de celui qui aime ce que l'âme est au corps qu'elle anime* (A 77, 576).

We might even risk going further by suggesting that '*la part du salon*' may be recovered if we remove the coating of cynicism, of what is faintly shocking, that we may presume LR liked to give to his formulations. One can imagine his pleasure in a pastime which may not have been taken as seriously as the *Maximes* are now taken. There is no evidence that certain 'shocking' statements were not whimsically meant. Gratitude, for instance, was perhaps amusingly described as 'an aid to trade', or the refusal to use cosmetics as one more kind of face-paint. How seriously did LR himself, or his circle of friends, take the suggestion (65) that prudence, though greatly praised, may not be effective? This is something that scholars cannot tell us.

I do not myself think that any social group, especially one operating under the inhibitions and conventions of a Paris salon in 1660, would be able to produce remarks as keen and clever as many of the Maximes which seem to belong to social conversation. Many silly things must have been said, as many have been written later about them. After all, LR thought that intelligent people need fools alongside them if social harmony is to be maintained. The *Maximes*, indeed, show habitual use of criteria which may not have occurred so prominently in the actual salon. They compare degrees of activity, small with great, few words with many. What is more important, they compare, in far too many cases to be mere echoes of conversation, appearance and reality, the idea and the fact, the name and the thing. Evidence for this will be gathered as we proceed.

Let us say that it is probable that the salon discussed the so-called virtues or good qualities. And after the virtues, the passions. This in itself would set quite a large programme of talking-points. On a rough count, over sixty Maximes in the standard text are on the subject of love. No less than eleven appear in sequence in what may be the oldest version of all (H). Perhaps the study of such a 'cluster' may take us as far back as we may go into the history of LR's epigrams. In the first edition they were split up, and later some were removed. They clearly move in the grooves of probable salon conversations, as one may see if one reads them together in any text of H. Love is compared to friendship; its power contrasted with that of indolence, its effect on the body with that on the mind. One epigram, removed by LR from his last edition, starts from the bondage of love, as so many sonnets have done, and ends with the neat reflection that, since we are not free to love or to cease from love, nobody need complain if a lady is fickle, or if a lover has more than one lady (577). A salon session might end with agreement that love can be neither hid nor copied (70), though this may be due to the moralist. Others in this group seem to me quite impenetrable: constancy is a misnomer and really its opposite (175). Or rather, constancy may be one of two things, an effect of duty, or of real love (176), just as inconstancy may be the name we give to philandering or to lack of interest (181). One wonders if it was by chance that this cluster of Maximes (which are not all strictly Maximes) is preceded by an attempt at definition, which we have already considered (68), and by the observation that pure love, if it really exists, is so deep in the heart that it cannot be seen (69). The sense that reflections of this kind may be quite close to actual conversations finds some support in those later removed. Since these are not, like many of the *maximes supprimées*, shocking in themselves, they were presumably claimed by other authors. Very few in this group suggest great profundity; many suggest the give and take of views in conversation. Perhaps the theme of love, as the *précieux* had captured it, was a subject on which LR had little of his own that he wished to say. He was content to play with formulas (as it were, practising on his instrument) suggested by others and likely to be to their taste.

One of the qualities for which Mme de Sablé was praised was her alliance of kindness and penetration. She encouraged everyone to speak, yet herself *pénétrait le fond de chaque chose* (*apud* Ivanov, p. 77). It is not surprising that in such a case in such a polite circle the talk should centre on the quality of politeness. If *Le Misanthrope* is (as has been suggested) a comedy on the subject of politeness, its merits and demerits, its perils and its value, then the *Maximes* supply useful contemporary comment on Molière's play. The ideal, as we know from many texts, is that of the *honnête homme*, but we need to remember that this expression stressed neither honesty nor masculinity, but rather considerate behaviour, and applied to women as well as to men. The *honnête homme*, in the *Maximes* as no doubt in the salons, was a man who did not take things in bad part and who was open about his shortcomings, not one who had nothing to conceal but one who did not appear as other than he was (155, 206). The *art de plaire* in such a company, which was seen in the women even more than in the men, did not depend on looks, or even on wit, but on the absence of monotony, on the way things were said rather than on what was said. Of Louis XIV, the idol and the model of that society, Saint-Simon, an enemy, was later to write: *Jamais homme si naturellement poli, ni d'une politesse si fort mesurée, si fort par degrès, ni qui distinguât mieux l'âge, le mérite, le rang. . . .* So politeness could be many things, a code, a topic, an ideal. But where the salon was probably content to note the effects, to compare attitudes, the *moraliste* sees and goes further. For him politeness is a paradox, since it is the opposite of that self-love which seems to be basic to all human action. The secret of charm in conversation was just to know how to listen. The reason why so many people are boring is that they are not listening, they are planning their next remarks (139). Knowing how to listen means studying one's company and realizing that some company like what other company will not like, as a later reflection puts it: *toute sorte de conversation, quelque honnête et quelque spirituelle qu'elle soit, n'est pas également propre à toute sorte d'honnêtes gens.* This means that the *honnêtes gens* are those who know when not to speak, who distinguish in fact between different sorts of silence: *Il y a un silence éloquent; il sert quelquefois à approuver et à condamner; il y a un silence moqueur; il y a un silence respectueux . . . (RD,* 4). The Maximes tend to suggest that conversation, the means of polite intercourse, is always artificial because, if it were not, then society would be split apart rather than knit together. We must, in society, respect others, quite apart from what we feel or wish within ourselves. *La complaisance est nécessaire dans la société, mais elle doit avoir des bornes; elle devient une servitude quand elle est excessive (RD,* 2). In fact LR assumes in polite speech a give and take, and surely it was the social group in which he moved that must have taught him this. He would have been as horrified as any salon *habitué* to hear an Alceste say

> Je veux . . . qu'en toute rencontre
> Le fond de notre cœu dans nos discours se montre

—for he knew that man's heart is evil. He never forgets, as Alceste's creator never allows us to forget, what he called *la malignité de notre nature.* Politeness he therefore regarded as an artificial and necessary covering thrown over *amour-propre,* and delighted in watching the real human emerge through his self-imposed disguise: *Quelque soin que l'on prenne de couvrir ses passions par des apparences de piété et d'honneur, elles paraissent toujours au travers de ces voiles* (12).

6. The Critique of Intelligence

᛭᛭᛭

Le goût de l'observation psychologique est un fruit de la vie mondaine. M. Ivanov comes to this conclusion after a study of the Vallant papers, which are full of evidence concerning the part played by *esprit* in the salons, in particular that of Mme de Sablé. That lady was repeatedly praised for her psychological acumen, for her skill in penetration and expression. One of Doctor Vallant's dossiers bears a title which could stand for others and for many of the Maximes: '*Pensées de M. Esprit sur l'esprit.*' This punning title is typical of a select society in which witty expression was both valued and cultivated. Here as elsewhere, LR seems to bring to perfection a gift displayed all around him. In her novel *Le Grand Cyrus* Mlle de Scudéry has this to say of Parthénice, Princesse de Salamis, who is said to be Mme de Sablé: *Jamais personne n'a si parfaitement connu toutes les différences de l'amour que la Princesse les connaît . . . ses distinctions* (*apud* Ivanov, p. 38). Differences and distinctions seem to have gone along with the wit and the conversation in the circle in which the *Maximes* were produced.

But few words are more elusive, three hundred years after the event, than '*esprit*'. The term is used both for that part of us which thinks, one might say the 'mind', and for the neat expression in words of that thinking. Yet we can hardly ever translate *esprit* by 'mind', since we are dealing with a society in which psychology as we know it did not exist. The Renaissance had the term 'wit', for the product of sharp thinking, but it was not wit that was deceived by the heart. If we are to avoid anachronism

in our judgements, if we are not to import an English
sense into a French concept, or a twentieth-century sense
into seventeenth-century words, we must wait until by
chance the actual users define their terms. By good fortune LR has in fact done this, in one of his unpublished
Réflexions. Not only so, but he has there admitted that he
and his contemporaries were far from clear as to what
exactly was the shade of meaning carried by terms
frequently used. He distinguishes the various kinds of
mind suggested by such terms as *grand esprit, bel esprit,
esprit adroit, bon esprit, esprit utile, esprit fin*. The tendency
in all of these is to describe a person, not a faculty, an
attitude embodied, not a part or facet of intelligence. Even
the grammar is doubtful: *Bien que toutes les qualités de
l'esprit se puissent rencontrer dans un grand esprit, il y en a néanmoins qui lui sont propres et particulières* (Éd. Pléiade, p. 531).

As in England it was a compliment to be called 'a man
of much wit', so in France we find the quality insisted on.
Rapin said of LR what the King said to Mme de Sévigné
about Racine, that *il avait beaucoup d'esprit*. Did this mean
a man skilled in expression, or in perception? Perhaps a
man both clever and pungent. LR himself professes not
to know: *Avoir beaucoup d'esprit est un terme équivoque; il
peut comprendre toutes les sortes d'esprit dont on vient de parler
mais il peut aussi n'en marquer aucune distinctement . . . on
peut avoir beaucoup d'esprit et n'être propre à rien, et avec beaucoup d'esprit on est souvent fort incommode*. (Was this Réflexion
written before or after Maxime 451?)

Clearly salon discussions ranged round such points as
these: the definition of intelligence, penetration, judgement, and the degree to which clever formulation of these
qualities could both illustrate and define them. Behind
Maxime 106 (quoted above, p. 35), for example, may have
been much animated discussion. If LR really wrote it,
then we have not been fair to what Matthew Arnold
would have called his imaginative reason. To see in the

early version merely a jumping-off point, so to say, for the extraction of two Maximes is to neglect a most suggestive line of thought. The comparison with medicine is, in mid-seventeenth century, suggestive. Just as medical phenomena were recorded and not related or co-ordinated, so were isolated features of human behaviour. But was not the succeeding age, the age of Voltaire, to do just this, to observe and to co-ordinate evidence which lack of proper instruments had prevented from being systematized? Is not this a pre-Enlightenment statement? Is it not the observation of a man who knew both Descartes and Pascal, and their contemporaries, at first hand, and who would agree with the one that we needed much more observation, and with the other that the new findings must be fitted into a new and larger scheme than scholasticism, or even Cartesianism, could furnish?

If in the light of this reflection we read the series of Maximes numbered 97–108 in the standard text, we may follow what must have been a wide-ranging discussion. To speak of a polite mind would now convey nothing, yet No. 99 refers to this. Perhaps we should think of 'an elegant attitude' or 'a civilized mind'? What is often called 'French politeness' seems to be defined in No. 100.

The distinction between *esprit* and *cœur* seems to cover, as in Pascal, the difference between conscious thinking and unconscious decision. One would like to say that the will is thought of as conscious, and *le cœur* as an alignment of the personality affecting the will, which occurs, like other internal physical changes, unknown and in secret. But LR himself discovered this in the Maxime which suggests that we are far from knowing all that we really intend. It is interesting to speculate whether LR ever listened to Pascal on the subject of the heart's having its reasons of which the reason knows nothing. But both men seem to have been of the same mind, as expressed in Maximes 102, 103, and 108.

On matters of terminology they seem to have differed. *Finesse* for Pascal seems to have been close to intuition and to have been a quality which he greatly respected. Not so LR. He calls *finesse* the mark of a small mind (125). The Pascalian sense he keeps for the expression '*un esprit fin*'; the abstract noun seems to stand in the *Maximes* for what is merely clever, as opposed to the really clever, *habileté*.

Un esprit fin et un esprit de finesse sont très différents. Le premier plaît toujours; il est délié, il pense des choses délicates, et voit les plus imperceptibles. Un esprit de finesse ne va jamais droit: il cherche des biais et des détours pour faire réussir ses desseins; cette conduite est bientôt découverte; elle se fait toujours craindre et ne mène presque jamais aux grandes choses.

These last words suggest an ambiance which is nearer to Retz than to Pascal. LR's picture of men was bound up with civil war. Pascal's acquaintances, as we come to know them from Professor Mesnard's picture of the Roannez circle, were probably more worthy, idealistic, animated by a principle of integrity which LR seems not to have met.

In one respect LR goes beyond Pascal, and that is in suggesting the way *cœur* may be said to occur in artistic inspiration, perhaps also in conversation: *Il y a de jolies choses que l'esprit ne cherche point, et qu'il trouve tout achevées en lui-même, de sorte qu'il semble qu'elles y soient cachées, comme l'or et les diamants dans le sein de la terre.* I do not understand how the inventor of this splendid reflection could be a cynic, however great his misfortunes. While it may have been in the interests of epigram to remove the image, the thought itself seems more complete and suggestive in its early form (quoted from L 133).

Behind all these reflections on intelligence may be a close reading of Montaigne. Like him, LR reserves his real admiration not for wit or skill, but for judgement.

Judgement, says No. 97, is not anything other than wit, but a profusion of it. The habit of mind which disregards incidentals, which perceives the obscure, this is judgement, a shining intellectual light (*la grandeur de la lumière de l'esprit*)—one does not know whether the metaphor is dead, a mere *façon de parler*, or is brought to life in the Racinian manner. Judgement, LR wrote later, is that quality which prevents you from being a fool (456). It has more to do with the formation of taste than has the intelligence (258). It is true reason, the reason that goes along with discernment, knowledge, and taste (105). It is the quality which chooses the right perspective, which looks at men and things from their true vantage-point (104).

A French concept is always better understood if one looks, as comedy encourages us to look, at its absence, at the opposed concepts. LR seems to have devoted as much care to the scrutiny of folly as he did to that of wit. Here again terms have changed their meaning. An Englishman should not presume to discern the nuances in the seventeenth-century use of *folie*, *niaiserie*, and *sottise*. LR himself altered *sot* to *fol* in his first edition. He more than once suggests the interaction of skill and folly, *Il arrive quelquefois des accidents dans la vie, d'où il faut être un peu fou pour se bien tirer* (310); *L'esprit nous sert quelquefois à faire hardiment des sottises* (415).

Wise living must take account of, and include, folly: *La folie nous suit dans tous les temps de la vie. Si quelqu'un paraît sage, c'est seulement parce que ses folies sont proportionnées à son âge et à sa fortune* (207. Note the variant of L: *L'enfance nous suit . . .*). Wisdom is not a common quality. Most of us can manage to be wise in matters where we are not affected: *Il est plus aisé d'être sage pour les autres que de l'être pour soi-même* (132; see also 591). We do not like to be reminded of our real limitations. LR gives us two forms of this remark, both culled from his classical reading (92, A 104).[1] In fact, folly is socially indispensable. A society of wise men would be intolerable: *Un homme d'esprit serait souvent embarrassé sans la compagnie des sots* (140). Again, no hint of cynicism, a Maxime in the finest sense, a beautiful form given to a single penetrating expression, so that the maximum of surprise and charm may be created in the reader who comes unprepared upon something he can enjoy but could not invent. One of the many forms of paradox in the making of Maximes is that they seem final, but are really a provocation to further reflection. Not for nothing did La Fontaine admire La Rochefoucauld:

> . . . il faut laisser
> Dans les grands sujets quelque chose à penser.

It is, as the poet well knew, an understatement.

The thinking behind the *Maximes* is of course unsystematic. *Monsieur de La Rochefoucauld n'avait pas étudié.* Thank goodness. Art has its reasons the mind knows nothing of. We must take him as we find him, like any other artist. Some of his observations may seem trite, such as the statement that some people need many words to say little (142). But his roving eye knew a small mind from a large (265, 502), and at times, without warning, of course, for that is a condition of writing Maximes, he

[1] Comparison with the source suggests why LR, in his third edition, recast his version of 1665:

The story is in Aelian (*Varia Historia*, iv. 25, and *Athenaeus*, xii. 81, p. 554 E). Athenaeus says it is from Heraclides Ponticus, a pupil of Plato, in his book on pleasure.

'Thrasyllus of Aexone was so mad that he thought that all the ships arriving at Piraeus were his. He made lists of them, arranged for their despatch and management, and welcomed them on their return as joyfully as if they had really been his, but without ever grieving for those which were lost. His brother Criton, visiting him from Sicily, put him into the doctor's hands and he was cured; but often afterwards he recalled his madness and said he had never been so happy as at the safe return of ships which had nothing to do with him.'

(I am grateful to my colleague Mr. D. A. Russell for this information.)

will convey a kind of judgement perhaps only possible to a Molière or to an autodidact, far from the schools. Like Montaigne he had an acute sense of what was called '*l'échec*', the point at which the mind is stopped, checked, ineffective. This may be due to us: *Nous avons plus de paresse dans l'esprit que dans le corps* (487). Or it may be due to others, who are not interested when we think they should be interested: *nous ne pouvons pardonner à ceux que nous ennuyons* (end of 304). LR seems able to follow our thoughts and our behaviour to the point where they get out into the world, so to say, and meet other forces: interests so many and so vast that they drown our few poor virtues, as rivers get lost in the sea.[1] In a happy revelation he once pictures the mind as unhindered, having, as Halifax said, its full flight, capable of infinite refinement and discipline. It is a Cartesian flash. In the *Discours de la méthode* Descartes had foreseen a day when men working in concert would make themselves masters of nature. LR does not go quite so far, but he suggests something even more remarkable: *L'esprit s'attache par paresse et par constance à ce qui lui est facile ou agréable. Cette habitude met toujours des bornes à nos connaissances, et jamais personne ne s'est donné la peine d'étendre et de conduire son esprit aussi loin qu'il pourrait aller* (482).

[1] A quotation from a kindred spirit may help us to see that LR is writing within the tradition of the great French *moralistes*. Benjamin Constant, who was surely among his perceptive readers, was to write: 'Il n'y a point d'unité complète dans l'homme, et presque jamais personne n'est tout-à-fait sincère, ni tout-à-fait de mauvaise foi' (*Adolphe*, ed. Rudler, p. 16). Compare Maxime 170: 'Il est difficile de juger si un procédé net, sincère et honnête est un effet de probité ou d'habileté.' Compare also Alison Fairlie's comment on the Constant passage, *French Studies*, xx, 1966, p. 231.

7. Political Implications[1]

༚༖༚

La pente vers soi est le commencement de tout
désordre, en guerre, en police, en économie (Br.
minor, 477).

WHAT Pascal has here in mind is what LR calls *amour-
propre*, but the *Maximes* do not often, if ever, suggest the
actual issues of politics. Was their author aware of them?
What in fact is the relation between social theory and the
Maximes? They have usually been read as non-political,
as temperamental reactions to, and statements of, egoism.
I hope to show in this chapter that their thought-world
is close to that of Hobbes and Retz, and furthermore that
they played some part in allowing the Enlightenment to
develop a social theory of which there is no trace in LR
himself. It may well be that suggestions about the nature
of man and of society, which LR handed on to Adam
Smith and Bentham, and they in turn to Marx, whatever
their intrinsic importance, help us to understand how
the modern world was made out of the hierarchic society
of the seventeenth century.

It is one of the contentions of this book that the *Maximes* are generalized statements of personal and particular
experience. We have seen that the art of the Maxime is
to express without local or temporal attachment a truth
arrived at in a particular situation, usually that of civil
war. In origin, therefore, the *Maximes* are close to
politics, and to social disruption. *Les 'Maximes'*, wrote

[1] Much of the material of this chapter appeared in *French Studies*, vii
(1953), 335–45.

Daniel Mornet, *ne sont pas seulement le divertissement d'un honnête homme, mais une expérience humaine et pathétique* (*Histoire de la littérature française classique*, 1947, p. 367). The world of the *Maximes* is in essentials the world of Hobbes, whose thought in *De Cive* and the *Leviathan* was worked out in France during the Fronde. The *Leviathan* in particular contains admirable descriptions of *amour-propre*. This should not surprise us, since Hobbes, like LR, describes a world where men do things because of fear and pride, rather than on principles of reason and morality:

> I put for a general inclination of mankind a perpetual and rest-less desire for power after power, that ceaseth only in death. And the cause of this is not always that a man hopes for a more intensive delight than he has already attained to, but because he cannot assure the power and means to live well, which he hath present, without the acquisition of more. (Ch. xi.) [And again:] [All society] is either for gain or for glory: that is, not so much for love of our fellows as for the love of ourselves.

This is not, with Hobbes, as it would be with Pascal and Port-Royal, a description of sin, or even a lamenta-tion on *la misère de l'homme*. It is a social datum, which springs from the natural desire for self-preservation: 'The dispositions of men are naturally such that, except they be restrained through fear of some coercive power, every man will distrust and dread each other . . . toward the preservation of himself' (*De Cive*, ed. Lamprecht, 1949, p. 11). Compare with this view an early reflection which had to be removed from the first editions, surely for obvious reasons, No. 578:

> La justice n'est qu'une vive appréhension qu'on ne nous ôte ce qui nous appartient; de là vient cette considération et ce respect pour tous les intérêts du prochain, et cette scrupu-leuse application à ne lui faire aucun préjudice. Cette crainte

retient l'homme dans les bornes des biens que la naissance ou la fortune lui ont donnés; et sans cette crainte [H : *pressé par la violente passion de se conserver*], il ferait des courses continuelles sur les autres.

It is strange that LR should have been singled out for his cynicism, while Hobbes, holding similar views, has been praised for his penetration. Their identity of view was no doubt due to the fact that they were looking at the same spectacle, French society in disruption. In that society it was probably no exaggeration to notice that 'there be very few, perhaps none, that in some cases are not blinded by self-love or some other passion' (*Leviathan*, Ch. xxvi).

The Fronde has sometimes been thought to be, as its name suggests, a make-believe war, but the original documents dispel this impression. The French nobles may have been playing at war in 1649, but they had the English tragedy before them. Mazarin was as unpopular as Laud had been, and perhaps even less protected than he was by laws and traditions of justice. He was quite conscious of the parallel: Retz quotes his statement that *le Parlement et les bourgeois et habitants de Paris étaient tous des Cromwell et des Fairfax qui en voulaient au roi et au sang royal pour faire comme en Angleterre et établir en France une république* (Retz, *Mémoires*, ed. Mongrédien, ii. 370).

One does not need to look far beneath the surface to see more tragedy than tragicomedy in the Fronde. The people, as Feillet showed long ago, suffered from every change of party. Conspiracy helped to deprive France of representative institutions for nearly 150 years. The intrigues may have been romanesque and scatter-brained, but nothing less was at stake than the unity and survival of the French State. The prospect of anarchy, explicit in Pascal's *Pensées*, was more than a politician's bogey: it meant a return to the conditions of only sixty years earlier.

The latest historian of the Fronde sees LR's writing as reflecting political ideas current in France in 1650:

> Si l'on suppose, comme il [LR] le fait, que même les passions aient un 'intérêt' et qu'il soit difficile d'y résister, si l'on suppose d'autre part que le hasard et la fortune conduisent la vie des hommes, qui se flattent de leurs grandes actions [cf. Maxime No. 7], on intègre dans un ensemble de forces aveugles et impersonnelles ces notions en origine si limitées et si rationnelles. L'amour-propre et l'intérêt obtiennent de cette façon une existence pour ainsi dire indépendante. Il n'y a plus personne qui possède un certain amour-propre ou qui vise à satisfaire ses intérêts; l'amour-propre et l'intérêt au contraire dominent des hommes incapables de les surmonter et aveuglément entraînés par des forces bien plus grandes qu'eux . . . cette ébauche d'une psychologie de caractère irrationnel répond exactement au développement de l'idée 'intérêt' dans la littérature politique du temps. (Kossmann, *La Fronde*, 1954, pp. 152–3.)

If this be a fair judgement we should regard the cynicism which is often attributed to LR as a feature of his age and his class. His contemporary Lenet wrote: *J'ai observé que l'intérêt est presque toujours la raison principale qui fait entrer les gens de qualité dans les partis.* For another, Mme de Motteville, self-interest was *le maître des cœurs, c'est celui qui gouverne le monde.* Quoting these statements, Kossmann sums up as follows: *L'idéal que poursuivaient les Frondeurs était un idéal de cynisme intéressé et de machiavélisme raffiné. . . . C'est comme si une épidémie d'égoïsme — et de l'égoïsme le plus étroit — sévissait dans le pays pendant quatre années tristes et chaotiques* (ibid., p. 151).

A convincing witness to all this is LR himself. His *Mémoires* are full of the comments of a man who is reflecting on many subjects which recur in the *Maximes*. It was a man who had dealt with Mazarin who was to write: *nous promettons selon nos espérances et nous tenons selon nos craintes* (Maxime 38). He had found that royal promises had no guarantee of being kept: *Mais tant de belles apparences n'éblouirent pas le Duc de LR; il dit en partant à M. le Duc d'Orléans que la sûreté de tant d'écrits et de tant de paroles si solennellement données dépendait du soin qu'on apporterait à garder le Palais Royal, et que la Reine se croirait dégagée de tout, du moment qu'elle serait hors de Paris.* Spanish promises were no less *vaines et trompeuses.* The advice of the Duc de Nemours was based less upon ambition than upon jealousy (cf. Maxime 7). Great persons are often ignorant of what is in their true interest.

The distinction between merit and fortune is a frequent theme of LR's *Mémoires*: *Néanmoins, comme la fortune règle les événements plus souvent que la conduite des hommes, elle fit rencontrer M. le Prince et le Coadjuteur dans le temps qu'ils se cherchaient le moins.* And again, of the Duc de Bouillon:

Son esprit était net, fertile en expédients et capable de démêler les affaires les plus difficiles . . . cependant, de si grands avantages lui furent souvent inutiles, par l'opiniâtreté de sa fortune, qui s'opposa presque toujours à sa prudence, et il mourut dans le temps que son mérite et le besoin que la Cour avait de lui auraient apparemment surmonté son malheur. (Cf. Maxime 65.)

But the *Mémoires* probably suggested more to the author of the *Maximes* than the interplay of intrigue and accident. LR had the advantage of comparing the Mazarins of his day with a really great man. He had no cause to love Richelieu, but certain Maximes suggest that he was in no doubt of the stature of his enemy, and used the great powers of Richelieu to assess the qualities of smaller men:

Il avait l'esprit vaste et pénétrant, l'humeur âpre et difficile; il était libéral, hardi dans ses projets, timide pour sa personne. Il voulut établir l'autorité du Roi et la sienne propre par la ruine des huguenots et des grandes maisons du royaume, pour attaquer ensuite la maison d'Autriche et abaisser une puissance si redoutable à la France. Tout ce qui n'était pas dévoué à ses volontés était exposé à sa haine, et il ne gardait point de bornes pour élever ses créatures ni pour perdre ses ennemis. (Éd. Pléiade, p. 35. Compare the more subtle but not greatly dissimilar portrait in Retz, ed. cit. i. 86 ff.)

If it was Richelieu who supplied a standard of judgement for LR, another gifted contemporary allows us to check the veracity and the psychology of LR's *Mémoires*. What the *Maximes* owe to the example and career of the Cardinal de Retz will never be known, but certainly in his person as in his book he challenges conventional morality no less directly and profoundly than does LR. Retz reveals in his own character, as in his remarks on other people, abundant proof that the self-interest and the vanity analysed in the *Maximes* are not the fantasies of *un cœur corrompu*, as Mme de La Fayette at first thought, but an actual feature of the men and the social class which both writers knew best. We might even go so far as to say that the vices laid bare in the *Maximes* are almost all illustrated in the person of Retz himself, who seems to accept the opportunist standards imposed by intrigue, and who is willing to reveal and display them almost without scruple or shame. Retz seems to treat life, as Sainte-Beuve remarked, as a drama, in which one has to play out one's role. He conveys in his writing the actor's illusion of life and action: *cela se sent comme la vie même* (ed. cit. i. 301). Although cast for the part of a churchman, he was, as he himself tells us, *l'âme peut-être la moins ecclésiastique qui fût dans l'univers*. He makes no secret of the fact that for him the Church had to be the way to power, and that piety was a cloak. He speaks of this assumed piety in terms as biting as those found in LR and Molière: *Il n'y a rien qui soit si juste sujet à l'illusion que la piété. Toutes sortes d'erreurs se glissent et se cachent sous son voile; elle consacre toutes sortes d'imaginations et la meilleure intention ne suffit pas pour y faire éviter les travers.*

The frankness and the subtlety of Retz were probably well known to LR. This fact makes a passage such as the following of possible importance for the *Maximes*:

Comme j'étais obligé de prendre les ordres, je fis une retraite à Saint-Lazare, où je donnai à l'extérieur toutes les apparences ordinaires. L'occupation de mon intérieur fut une grande et profonde réflexion, sur la manière que je devais prendre pour ma conduite. Elle était très difficile. Je trouvais l'archevêché de Paris dégradé, à l'égard du monde, par les bassesses de mon oncle, et désolé, à l'égard de Dieu, par sa négligence et par son incapacité. Je prévoyais des oppositions infinies à son rétablissement; et je n'étais pas si aveugle, que je ne connusse que la plus grande et la plus insurmontable était dans moi-même. Je n'ignorais pas de quelle nécessité est la règle des mœurs à un évêque. Je sentais que le désordre scandaleux de ceux de mon oncle me l'imposait encore plus étroite et plus indispensable qu'aux autres; et je sentais en même temps que je n'en étais pas capable, et que tous les obstacles de conscience et de gloire que j'opposerais au dérègle-ment ne seraient que des digues fort mal assurées. Je pris, après six jours de réflexion, le parti *de faire le mal par dessein, ce qui est sans comparaison le plus criminel* devant Dieu, mais ce qui est sans doute le plus sage devant le monde; et parce qu'en le faisant ainsi l'on y met toujours des préalables, qui en cou-vrent une partie; et parce qu'on évite par ce moyen le plus dangereux ridicule qui se puisse rencontrer dans notre pro-fession, qui est celui de mêler à contre-temps le péché dans la dévotion. (Éd. Pléiade, p. 47.)

I suggest that this passage has more than autobio-graphical interest. It is a picture of the standards and values which came to the surface of conduct in the Fronde. What Retz illustrates in his own person, the *Maximes* constantly analyse. Expediency and necessity have, in that political context in which both Retz and LR were involved, the deciding voice. Indeed, there seemed to be no other means of holding one's ground in a combative society. Those who wished to survive had to adopt a new standard, and Retz was proud of it. He underlined in his manuscript the words italicized above and there is no better expression of his *Realpolitik*. Thus he delights to quote speeches in which he had to profess what was the official morality. He invents quotations to give his words more weight, and to display himself as the noblest Roman of them all. *Dans les mauvais temps, je n'ai point abandonné la ville; dans les bons je n'ai point eu d'intérêts; dans les désespérés, je n'ai rien craint.* Yet this pseudo-morality was also policy, designed to win adherents, and apparently did so. Nevertheless, it produced on the part of those who were not misled, those who saw through the profession of morality, a reaction of scepticism, defiance, and constant watchfulness. This reaction is implicit in the *Maximes*: *On ne saurait compter toutes les espèces de vanité*, etc. Being forced to fight against one's friends more often than against one's enemies made it more difficult to conduct a conspiracy than a campaign, to lead a faction than an army. Their experience in the context of plot and scheme and face-saving has accustomed both men to the double standard. Knowing that virtue was paraded as often as it was sincere, they could not assume any profession of virtue to be true. The real cause of both speech and act might be vicious, or imposed by the necessity for self-preservation.

The numerous coincidences of detail in the work of the two men need not be recounted here. Their proper place is in a critical edition of the *Maximes*. The essential point is that, when checked by the *Mémoires* of both Retz and LR, the world of the *Maximes* is seen as one of the most corrupt in modern society. It is a world in which virtue is still professed but in which deceit and pride lead the dance, in which altruism is superfluous, almost ridiculous, since self-interest has to come first. Yet in that world admirable qualities are required: presence of mind, courage, intelligence, decision, 'elevation'

(whatever that elusive word may mean). Both writers
agree that these qualities count; both have watched them
displayed by contemporaries.
Yet there is, perhaps, one essential difference between
the attitudes of the two men. For LR, in the *Maximes* at
least, the quality summed up in the word 'truth' is of great
importance. The author is concerned to see, and to say,
what is true about behaviour. Retz makes many true
observations, but he is even more concerned than was
LR in his *Mémoires* to make his case and to draw an
impressive self-portrait. In doing this he shows what
has been called 'a frivolity, in respect of truth and sincerity, which makes one shudder'. One who had spent
years in study of the documents judged that Retz's work
was full

of misrepresentations, travesties, intentional silences and omissions, denials, subterfuges, narration that bears the outward
stamp of veracity yet is in reality complete fabrication, alterations in facts and dates with intent to mislead, admissions of
faults which seem to be due to the greatest frankness and which
turn out to be artifice with a view to hiding even worse
faults, of terrible accusations which spring back upon the
accuser. There is no sort of swindling and artifice that Retz
has not employed in order to show himself to posterity as
entirely different from what he was to his contemporaries.
(R. Chantelauze, in Retz, *Œuvres*, Éd. Grands Écrivains, ix.
iii. Quoted by G. Misch in a valuable article, 'Die Auto-
biographie der französischen Aristokratie des 17. Jh.', *Viertel-
jahrschrift für Literatur und Geistesgeschichte*, i. 172–213.)

There was also significant difference of outlook. In
some respects LR does not share the viewpoint of Retz.
His opportunism, his readiness to sacrifice principle to
expediency, above all his empirical attitude, as seen for
instance in the *Conjuration de Fiesque*, are not, I think,
found in the *Maximes*. LR is more concerned to point
the difference between accepted morality and actual

practice. The main emphasis of the two writers is thus quite different. But we may think of Retz as the most immediate and incisive personal force behind the *Maximes*. To have in one's own circle an intriguer of the stature and the resource of Retz must have sharpened LR's own challenge to conventional morality.

It is therefore likely that the *Maximes* reflect a distinctive political milieu. We should think of their publication as a revelation to the public of attitudes which many remembered from the years of civil war, and which must have appeared to run counter both to religious orthodoxy and to the philosophy of a settled society. But for those who still had in mind the events of the Fronde they must have recalled the outburst of cynical egoism which seemed to be a mark of that time.

The first scholar to appreciate this relationship seems to have been Sainte-Beuve. In his study of 1840, which represented his personal breakthrough to a new kind of criticism, he came to see LR less as a classical writer and more as a great outsider, a man holding moral explosive, and an artist who cultivated a form of expression cold and objective enough to contain matter which, unadorned and unveiled, would have seemed shocking and disruptive. *Par un long commerce avec le livre trop relu*, Sainte-Beuve had learned to read the *Maximes* in depth, so to speak, not as a book of morals but as a picture of fallen man, of *la misère de l'homme*: *L'homme de La Rochefoucauld est exactement l'homme déchu. . . . Les réflexions morales de LR semblent vraies, exagérées ou fausses, selon l'humeur et la situation de celui qui les lit. Elles ont droit de plaire à quiconque a eu sa Fronde et son coup de feu dans les yeux.* In a later study Sainte-Beuve suggested that this moral climate of the Fronde had affected others of the same generation:

> Bossuet n'a si bien peint, dans leur ensemble moral du moins, et dans leur aspect terrible et majestueux, les grands orages d'Angleterre qu'il n'avait pas vus et dont le sens politique lui

échappait que parce qu'il avait observé de près chez nous ces temps d'ébranlement où toutes les notions du devoir sont renversées, et où les meilleurs perdent la bonne voie. ('De la connaissance de l'homme au xviie siècle', *N.L.*, iii. 228.)

The *Maximes*, then, to be rightly read must be seen as the offshoot of the political and moral upheaval of the Fronde. But their political implications are not bounded by this fact of their origin. On the contrary, their effect was possibly even more political than their cause. One would not surmise this to be so from, for instance, Voltaire, one of their great admirers, who once said that the book taught the French nation to think, and indicated by the context that he meant also to express their thoughts in a pungent manner (*Le Siècle de Louis XIV*, Éd. Hachette, p. 624). But modern research has revealed unsuspected affinities between Jansenist writing and the optimism which we associate with the Enlightenment. In particular Professor Raymond, of Geneva, was able to show in a remarkable study that *les sources de la sociologie optimiste des 'philosophes' doivent être cherchées, pour une part dans la sociologie pessimiste du 17e siècle, et qu'une morale chrétienne sombre, préoccupée de pourchasser l'amour-propre dans ses derniers re-tranchements, a contribué à engendrer par réaction une morale fondée sur l'intérêt.*

The new direction would seem to start, or at least to become explicit, as with so many others of the seventeenth century, in the work of Thomas Hobbes. In his treatise *On the Citizen* he accepts LR's basic assumption that self-love is dominant in all men, and suggests that true polity can be built upon this basis, and that it is in the interest of all of us to limit our self-interest. The thought is taken up in the Jansenist camp by both Pascal and Nicole. The former notes that *on tirerait de la concupiscence des règles admirables de police*, and the latter, in a series of essays which appeared from 1671 onwards, tried to spell out this polity. One of these essays bore the significant title: '*De la Charité et de l'Amour-Propre*'. It contained a new formula: *Pour réformer entièrement le monde, c'est-à-dire pour en bannir tous les vices et tous les désordres grossiers, et pour rendre les hommes heureux dès cette vie même, il ne faudrait, au défaut de la charité, que leur donner à tous un amour-propre éclairé, qui sût discerner ses vrais intérêts* (*apud* M. Raymond, 'Du jansénisme à la morale de l'intérêt', *Mercure de France*, juin 1957, pp. 238–55).

This enlightened self-interest is found in Mandeville, and in many of the eighteenth-century thinkers who read *The Fable of the Bees*: in Voltaire, in Helvétius, in Adam Smith. M. Raymond discerns, indeed, a new type of reader in the later seventeenth century: *Cet homme nouveau a lu Pascal, il a entendu parler de Hobbes, il a médité La Rochefoucauld et ses 'Maximes'. Tous l'invitent à compter avec l'égoïsme humain, et même à croire que de cet égoïsme peut sortir le bonheur de la société.*

Among these newly oriented readers I think that perhaps a special place in any work on the *Maximes* should be given to Helvétius, and in particular to the passage cited by M. Raymond:

> Lorsque le célèbre M. de La Rochefoucauld dit que l'amour-propre est le principe de toutes nos actions, combien l'ignorance de la vraie signification de ce mot amour-propre ne souleva-t-elle pas de gens contre cet illustre auteur? On prit l'amour-propre pour orgueil et vanité; et l'on s'imagina en conséquence que M. de La Rochefoucauld plaçait dans le vice la source de toutes les vertus. Il était cependant facile d'apercevoir que l'amour-propre, ou l'amour de soi, n'était autre chose qu'un sentiment gravé en nous par la nature, que ce sentiment se transformait dans chaque homme en vice ou en vertu, selon les goûts et les passions qui l'animaient, et que l'amour-propre différemment modifié produisait également l'orgueil et la modestie. La connaissance de ces idées aurait préservé M. de La Rochefoucauld du reproche tant répété qu'il voyait l'humanité trop en noir; il l'a connue telle qu'elle est. (*Apud* Raymond, art. cit., p. 251.)

This acute judgement suggests that many people had found as early as 1750 a way of reading LR which seems to make more sense than the way in which many people still read him. The work of modern scholars in the field of political and social theory suggests that the *Maximes* are significant within a wide context of seventeenth-century speculation. They should be read, not as the disappointed experiences of a cynic, but as seminal investigations into the causes of human behaviour. Much more is at stake here than an individual judgement of good and bad qualities. Hobbes, says a recent writer, 'saw society as so necessarily fragmented by the struggle of each for power over others that all were equal in insecurity'. Such an attitude was no part of the feudal conception of property, and in England 'it had grown to the point where it could be held responsible for the Civil War' (C. B. Macpherson, *The Political Theory of Possessive Individualism*, O.U.P. paperback ed., pp. 93, 64).

Hobbes and those who thought on the same lines as he did were thus led to a new concept of power. If 'the capacity of every man to get what he wants is opposed by the capacity of every other man' (op. cit., p. 36), then this fact, and not any external precept or principle, forces on men an obligation based on their self-interest:

In thus deriving right and obligation from fact, Hobbes was taking a radically new position. He was assuming that right did not have to be brought in from outside the realm of fact, but that it was there already . . . a leap in political theory as radical as Galileo's formulation of the law of uniform motion in natural science, and not unrelated to it. In each case a revolutionary change was initiated by a simple shift in assumptions. (Macpherson, op. cit., p. 76.)

If for Hobbes we read LR and for the English Civil War we read the Fronde, then we begin to see the extreme originality of the *Maximes* in the history of European ideas.

8. The Maxime as Art Form

𝐖𝐇𝐀𝐓 is a *sentence*? The answer to this question must be sought in the area of scholasticism. To know how the term was used in the Middle Ages is to begin to understand what the men of the seventeenth century inherited along with the word. One teacher says that in any writing we may find, and must not confuse, three things: the words, the open meaning, and the deep understanding: *Expositio tria continet: literam, sensum, sententiam. Littera est congrua ordinatio dictionum . . . sensus est . . . aperta significatio . . . sententia est profundior intelligentia.* Another teacher seeks in the *sententia* something not supplied by the speaker only, something objective, impersonal: *sententia est dictum impersonale.* Dante distinguished *littera* and *vera sentenzia.* This suggests why the expression *dare sententiam* carried the meaning not of an opinion so much as a judgement, with a suggestion of finality.[1]

To the contemporaries of LR the *sentence* suggested not only finality but, even more obviously, brevity. Another scholastic distinction is that between expansive writing, known as *amplificatio*, and contracted writing, known as *abbreviatio.* The second demanded no less effort and ingenuity than the first. As Horace had said,

> Brevis esse laboro
> Obscurus fio.

The effort to condense has been seen as a remedy for *taedium, fastidium*, produced by listening to many words.

[1] All these references are in G. Paré, *Le Roman de la Rose et la scolastique courtoise*, 1941.

The finest form of writing was epic narration, but it must have been a relief to turn to few and cogent words.[1] The obscurity, which for Horace was a fault, seems to have been cultivated, as an additional attraction. Proverbs and wise sayings are at times too metallic to be clear. The oracular, the Delphic word of wisdom, or of prophecy, was a dark word, mysterious rather than explicit. Rabelais recovered it in the final answer to Panurge: 'Trincq'. *Abbreviatio* can go no further; all possibilities of application are left open. Huizinga is of use to us here:

> The close connections between poetry and the riddle are never entirely lost. In the Icelandic skalds too much clarity is considered a technical fault. The Greeks also required the poet's word to be dark. Among the troubadours, in whose art the play function is more in evidence than in any other, special merit was attributed to the trobarclus, the making of recondite poetry. Modern schools of lyric which move and have their being in realms not generally accessible and are fond of wrapping the sense in enigmatic words are thus remaining true to the essence of their art. (J. Huizinga, *Homo Ludens*, 1949, p. 134.)

Were we not so accustomed to separate poetry and prose, to the extent of thinking that the matter of the one can never appear in the other, we should be free to read the *Maximes* as bearers of a long and complex cultural tradition. One of their enduring surprises indeed is that LR is able to turn a society amusement back into one of the highways of linguistic expression. In his letters he speaks of *sentences* as forms which emerge in the course of composition, and which are known as such not by the writer so much as by the reader. In an early reflection he suggests that the art of the *sentence* cannot be learned: *il est . . . ridicule de vouloir faire des sentences sans avoir la graine en soi* (505).

[1] See E. R. Curtius, *European literature and the Latin middle age*, Bonn, 1948, Excursus XIII.

Not of course that he needed to invent pungent speech.
Here again he was in a tradition. The Renaissance had
produced writing of metallic brevity, and, what is more,
had encouraged its cultivation. The *Adagia* of Erasmus,
published first in 1500, were among the best-sellers of
the century, and frequently showed a sense of the lapidary
alongside the explanatory. Montaigne, one of his most
devoted admirers, perhaps learned from Erasmus the
effectiveness of the paragraph which ends in a single
phrase, or a picture, thus enforcing an argument with
a pungent observation. This he would make at times
familiar: *Nous n'allons pas, on nous emporte* (III. 4); and at
times almost the reverse, teasing, complex as a conun-
drum: *La défence attire l'entreprise et la défiance l'offence* (end
of II. 15).

It was not only readers of Erasmus and Montaigne
who liked this sort of thing. Theatre-goers were trained
to expect it, and such a master of drama as Corneille
saw to it that they got plenty of what were sometimes
called *sentences* and which certain printers italicized so that
the gem of thought or expression should not be missed.
Thus, *Te perdre en me vengeant ce n'est pas me venger.* (The
paradox would apply not only to Cinna but to other
tragic figures, Roxane and Mithridate.) We know that
Pascal liked such brevity, and his *Pensées* show him to be
a master of this kind of expression. *Le cœur a ses raisons
que la raison ne connaît point*—is this not *abbreviatio* of a
distinguished kind? Let us remember that Pascal and
LR frequented the same salon.

It is clear then that LR was reviving an ancient form
of writing when in 1685 he made public the slim volume
of *Réflexions, ou Sentences et maximes morales*. Study cannot recover more than a general notion of the exact
resonance conveyed by each of these words in his title.
But we need not assume LR to have been entirely
ignorant of all his predecessors. He clearly read Mon-

taigne, possibly Erasmus also and Gracian, and he knew Latin: he quoted Juvenal with discrimination. Such knowledge in a writer who has gifts of brevity and pungency must have played its part in the production of the art form of modern epigram. We should not go far wrong if we considered *réflexions* as the loosest of the three words. Those *Réflexions diverses* which LR left unpublished show that brevity was not essential to their writing. The *sentence* he seems to have considered to be a single statement of a metallic or oracular kind, admitted by hearer or reader to be more than an individual opinion. The *Maxime* was probably not far from this. La Bruyère, with LR in mind, was to write that *les maximes sont comme des lois dans la morale*.

LR said in his Preface that he would not have published his work but for the appearance of a pirated edition, from *une méchante copie*. Perhaps we should be grateful for the incitement to publish, since the making of Maximes would seem to be an endless process. There are in LR's manuscripts reflections which are not Maximes, there are statements which are among the most famous of the *Maximes*, already perfect, as it were. And there are reflections which contain Maximes. The first edition shows the process in being, so to speak. Nobody could call its opening page a Maxime, nor its closing reflection. The mixture of *sentences* and *réflexions* can tell us much about the making of epigrams.

Nietzsche, the chief modern admirer of LR, thought that the beauty of the Maxime lay in the paradoxical blend of brevity in actual expression and wide range of meaning and suggestion. The result, according to him, was a gem of speech which could resist the passing of time and the change of fashion: *Eine gute Sentenz ist zu hart für die Zahn der Zeit und wird von allen Jahrtausenden nicht aufgezehrt, obwohl sie jeder Zeit zur Nahrung dient.* So that we should be mistaken in thinking of LR's art as being aimed only at tabloid speech. He can provide many kinds of pungency. Few words, which express much; musical words that suggest as well as convey meaning; intellectual comparisons, images, symbolic writing; all these are found. (Before we try to discover in what proportions, let us imagine how far they were expected by the first readers.) Clearly LR was attempting a definite kind of writing. He was not providing the same kind of entertainment as the writers of novels, of *mémoires*, of history, or of drama. He was in fact advertising, by his very title, his connection with other types of literary expression, all of which seem to have cultivated the hermetic, the obscure, the challenging; this literature did not so much offer something to be enjoyed as try to tease its readers into something to be deciphered. The point is made in the actual title of a work published twenty years before the *Maximes*: *L'Art de faire des Devises, où il est traité des hieroglyphes, symboles, emblèmes, aenigmes, sentences, paraboles, revers de medailles, armes, blasons, criniers, chiffres et rebus, avec un traité des rencontres ou mots plaisans.* This work suggests that *symbole* and *sentence* were of the same order of statement, that both managed to combine gravity and brevity, and thus attain a power of suggestion which ordinary statement could not do: . . . *le propre des Symboles est d'estre caché et envelopé dans des labyrinthes de sentences obscures . . . il faut qu'il y ait un grand sens compris sous la gravité et brièveté des Symboles . . . la brièveté donc conjointe à une certaine gravité qui comprend beaucoup de choses sous une même signification est le propre du Symbole.*[1]

The mark of the Maxime is form. A *réflexion* may have no recognizable form, but by compressing much material into few statements, it makes a Maxime possible. It is a mistake to judge Maximes by their truth. Whoever said

[1] It is interesting that the modern scholar from whom I take information about this book sees in it some prefiguration of Baudelaire's notions of symbol. See L. J. Austin, *L'Univers poétique de Baudelaire*, 1956, pp. 70, 73.

that the Maxime should express a statement with which we must all agree? This if logically applied would turn Maximes into truisms. Since they are clearly not this, we must ask what else the seventeenth-century reader could see or expect to see in the Maxime. The answer is, something directly opposed to a truism. 'Revelation' would be a better word. A grave and pregnant statement, which has power to shock and to startle, does not immediately appear as the truth. Its elusive and teasing suggestion is rather that of a new angle on the truth. In the case of LR's *Maximes* this statement is specifically directed to truths we are prevented from seeing because of our involvement in them. Rather than the truth, they present an aspect of truth, a way towards the truth, in particular a way to truths that are unwelcome, unpalatable, truths we are not likely to see unaided. Something of this emerges in an early reflection which has not quite the ring, the resonance, the form of a Maxime: *Ce qui nous empêche souvent de bien juger des sentences qui prouvent la fausseté des vertus, c'est que nous croyons trop aisément qu'elles sont véritables en nous* (517).

Let us see from a fresh sample the difference which form can make to a reflection which interests us by its content rather than by its form: *Le monde, ne connaissant point le véritable mérite, n'a garde de pouvoir le récompenser; aussi n'élève-t-il à ses grandeurs et à ses dignités que des personnes qui ont de belles qualités apparentes, et il couronne généralement tout ce qui luit, quoique tout ce qui luit ne soit pas de l'or* (L 165). Is it fanciful to see in the reflection an emerging Maxime? One can imagine the conversation which could go on, to and fro, around such a topic as the reward of merit. LR may well be noting a general agreement in the salon as to the frequency with which apparent merit seemed to secure rewards denied to true merit. Yet he did not publish this reflection, but a shorter one, giving the gist of it in thirteen words: *Le monde récompense plus souvent les apparences du mérite que le mérite même* (166). It would surely be unjust to call 166 a shortened version of L 165. The one has form and the other has not. By form we mean obvious and pleasing shape, a recurrence of sounds and a harmonious grouping of syllables. These ensure to the thought-content a sound-track, as it were, so that the statement is appreciated with leisure and pleasure. LR has discovered a way of saying less than L 165 says, of missing out some of its explicit statements and its ramificatory connectives: *aussi . . . que . . . et quoique,* even of sacrificing its cliché image. Yet the omission of all these things intensifies the power of expression, so that by saying less, 166 says more than L 165. Its single statement, standing unqualified, appears as a dense statement, in its own full potential. We may distinguish within it four implicit contrasts: *monde/mérite, apparences/mérite,* and *plus souvent* (implying *moins souvent*). These are made the more attractive by the recurrence in sound: the five M sounds and the inner rhyme of *récompense/apparences.*

We are not here confronted with obligatory form: no rule or custom lays down that a Maxime must have certain features. Certain Maximes (167 for instance) seem to have a minimum of form, neither echo nor rhyme, merely paradox within a short sentence, the more striking for the statement's being without qualification. But things are different in 169: *Pendant que la paresse . . .* and in 137: *On parle peu quand la vanité ne fait pas parler.* The enclosure of the statement between two forms of a single verb is probably not accidental, but even if it were, it is an artistic and formal achievement, since it conveys (symbolically?) something we hesitate to admit: most of the time we do not so much speak as are made to speak, by vanity, an agency we despise. It is not clear, from so abbreviated a statement, whether LR did or did not despise vanity. One might assume that he did not, since he took such trouble to respect its power. But that again is not the main point. To discuss, as many tend to do, the cynicism of this statement is to disregard its formal qualities. The omission of two in themselves insignificant words (*peu* and *pas*) would not greatly alter the sense, but it would disturb the form.

With the whole pageant of modern poetry before us, we may think simple cases of alliteration specious or naïve. This is not to say that the seventeenth century did so. Nor need we try to find exact explanations of dominant sounds: for example F may suggest a quality of *fausseté*, but also one of *fierté*. Perhaps we can do no more than be aware of alliterative features. Here are some striking examples:

Sound C	L'homme est conduit lorsqu'il croit se conduire . . . L 19
	Il condamne ses condamnations . . . L 108
	. . . qui peut connaître son cœur? L 233
	Ceux qui sont incapables de commettre de grands crimes . . . A 20 (611)
	La constance des sages . . . dans le cœur. 20
F	force/faiblesse 44 (and 122) La fortune . . . favorise. 60
	finesse/feindre 117 faudrait/fortune/fera 574 (A 74)
A and M	amour/âme/aime/anime 576 (A 77)
I	Notre défiance justifie la tromperie d'autrui. 86
-EUR	bonheur/malheur/humeur 61
-EUR/-EUX	heureux/malheureux 49
P	petitesse d'esprit/opiniâtreté L 235
	. . . personne ne se plaint . . . 89
PR	prudence/providence 65 (L 55)
PR, PL	. . . sous prétexte de pleurer une personne . . . nous pleurons. L 86
	. . . on pleure pour être pleuré . . . L 58

P and V	On peut . . . ce qu'on veut, pourvu qu'on le veuille bien. L 2
R	réputation/repos 205
S	. . . les plus sages le sont . . . 591
V	. . . en vieillissant, comme ceux du visage 112
	. . . nous nous vantons souvent . . . nous ne voulons pas nous trouver. 140
	vices/vertus 186, 189 vertu/vanité 200
	. . . vanité des vivants . . . 612

No less attractive than recurring sound is recurring accent. Read with deliberation, the finer Maximes fall into comparable groups, for which the practised reader learns to wait, and from which he receives a pleasure usually thought of as poetic. Indeed, the variations among these groups are closer to the rhythms of French verse than English people, accustomed to the set measures of English prosody, tend to imagine. We in England think and at times speak of the alexandrine as a monotonous measure, because it consists of twelve syllables, usually divided into two groups of six. But what the French ear waits for, and in fact hears, would be better described as four groups, in this case of three syllables each:

Captive/toujours triste/importune/à moi-même

But in this case of one, five, two, and four:

Ah/ne puis-je savoir/si j'aime/ou si je hais

And in this, of two and four and four and two:

J'ai dit/ce que jamais/on ne devait/entendre

It is more important to experience this variety than to explain it. Similarly with the *Maximes*. One of the attractions of No. 19 is that it can be read as four groups of four syllables:

Nous avons tous/assez de force/pour supporter/les maux d'autrui.

No. 42 falls into nearly the same groups with slightly more flexibility:

Nous n'avons pas assez de force pour suivre toute notre raison.

Rewarding to study, from all the points of view we have so far mentioned, is No. 49. Its earliest form would appear to be not yet a Maxime: *Les biens et les maux sont plus grands dans notre imagination qu'ils ne le sont en effet; et on n'est jamais si heureux ni si malheureux que l'on pense* (H 125). The link conjunction is worth notice. Does it add one observation to another, or offer an alternative expression of the first? The first statement is a fairly clear reminiscence of an early essay of Montaigne (I. 14). The second, with an alteration that I take to be significant, has made a Maxime:

On n'est jamais si heureux ni si malheureux qu'on s'imagine.

The existence of a variant (in H 128) suggests that the search for a satisfactory formulation was tentative.

Some have found in the *Maximes* near-alexandrines. No. 146 could be read as twelve prose syllables:

On ne loue d'ordinaire que pour être loué.

But No. 153 is hardly less pleasing, fifteen syllables which may be read as three groups of four and one of three. If we prefer, we may describe this as two statements of exactly similar grouping (3 and 4) linked by a neutral connective.

Many Maximes begin, as do alexandrines, with a hemistich, or group of six or seven syllables:

Plus on aime une maîtresse	111
Le refus des louanges	149
Quand les vices nous quittent	192
Il y a des rechutes	193
La parfaite valeur	216
L'intérêt met en œuvre	253
Le plaisir de l'amour	259
La fortune et l'humeur	435

This last, indeed, would seem to me one of the great formal successes of the collection. As read in prose it consists of two groups of three syllables forming the subject, followed by predicate and object of two syllables each. But the effect is not only of measure and balance, but of balance imposed on paradox. The vast range of suggestion opened up by the coupling of two qualities as ruling the world (where most readers would think of quite other powers as in command of affairs) administers that shock which is the privilege of epigram, conveying in rhythmical speech a view nobody would actually hold, yet which, when so expressed, is full of sense. If one were to say something of this kind in ordinary conversation, it might run: 'Talk as you will of King or *Conseil d'État*, in the last resort it is the conjunction of personal and temporal forces that achieves changes in the commonwealth, and these are a matter of temperament as well as of will'; and this might provoke the comment: 'An interesting idea, but rather far-fetched.' The Maxime, on the other hand, fascinates for ever. Somewhat in the same way Racine expresses distress in so perfect a formulation of sounds and groups that the hateful is made pleasing:

Tout m'afflige et me nuit et conspire à me nuire.

So far we have dealt only with accessory qualities of epigram. What happens when we set aside the pleasures of sound and rhythm and look at what we might term the *raison d'être* of epigram, the compression of speech? At times LR seems to achieve almost the ultimate degree of concision, and properly to judge his achievement we must ask how far speech can be compressed. The briefest possible sentence is perhaps a single predicate imperative: 'Fear not', 'Rejoice'. Proverbial speech is at times content with no more than a subject and a predicate: *Experientia docet*. But the maker of epigrams has to convey to

civilized people more than a saw or a saying, more than
trite wisdom. He has to use his few words to surprise,
shock, reveal, suggest. Blake can do this in four words:
'Energy is eternal delight.' LR needs a few more. In
six he can suggest two means of reckoning age, as a natural
span of time and as an art to be acquired: *Peu de gens
savent être vieux* (423). He can take three operative words:
défiance, justifie, tromperie, and add two particularizing
possessives to arrive at this: *Notre défiance justifie la tromperie d'autrui* (86).

Paradox is basic to epigram, but LR contrives to
suggest more than what is unusual and surprising. He
penetrates the contrast between appearance and reality
to the point of suggesting the mystery of all behaviour.
In a world where one is surrounded by others, what looks
like one thing may be its opposite: *Constance . . . est
inconstance* (175); *La vertu est un fantôme . . .* (L 187). *Folie*
may be *sagesse, sobriété* may be *impuissance de manger* (592,
593). To the quality we call love we may not be able to
give any precise content at all: *Il est malaisé de définir
l'amour. . .* (L 30).

This being so, comparison and contrast will be the
most frequent elements in a Maxime. It has not been
noticed that most of the *Maximes* convey, not a fact, nor
even an opinion, but a relation. It is relation, in the sense
of *rapport*, which turns a truism into an epigram: thus,
Les occasions nous font connaître aux autres—this everyone
knows—*et encore plus à nous-mêmes*. This is a shock, the
more perceptible for having been preceded by the ano-
dyne statement (345).

We must go carefully here, for we are in the region of
much of the best French classical writing. Comedy, irony,
satire all depend on contrast, on unemotional contrast,
presented by the mind as a comment on the world of
reality. Absolute statements are rare in the *Maximes*;
in the world of reality contrast, explicit or implicit, is

everywhere: this but not that, this less than that, this like that, past but not present, others but not us. Here we come upon one of the qualities of epigram, that it looks like simple statement, shorn of qualification and comparison. Yet it is so contrary to the reader's natural assumption that it provokes dissent, demur, contrast, comparison, difference. LR's apparent statements about death, for example, are all comparisons. Death is openly compared, to the sun (26). Attitudes to death are opposed: *Peu de gens* connaissent *la mort; on* . . . *la* souffre . . . (23). There is no need to repeat here epigrams in which mind is compared to body, to emotion; wit to folly. Paradox is seen to be close to contrast. It is a paradox of speech, for instance, that many words may say little, few may say much.

The most artistic use of paradox is seen in LR's handling of images, of physical pictures to illustrate moral conditions. Images are more frequent than one might think in the *Maximes*; most of them are not immediately startling, but ordinary. This is necessary if they are to convey an impression immediately. The governing factor of the epigram is time. 'A thought must tell quickly or not at all', said Hazlitt. The image is therefore usually limited to a single word, left unexplained. The perfect plain case is perhaps No. 380: *La fortune fait paraître nos vertus et nos vices comme la lumière fait paraître les objets.* As we reflect upon this formulation we see that the bare mention of light was sufficient. All the artist needs is to suggest a dark room; when light is admitted we see what all the time has been there, invisible. But that conduct should be so envisaged is shocking, to an age that has not known Freud. That our qualities, within us and as yet unknown, will be called forth by the chance encounters of our existence, is disturbing, and would not disturb so much if it were not left unexplained, with a single word and image as pointer.

The use of pictures of external nature is amazing. It allows the vast spaces of the sea, the mystery of the wind or of fire, to animate the briefest epigram. To describe the charm of novelty as bloom on fresh fruit is surely poetic: *La grâce de la nouveauté est à l'amour ce que la fleur est sur les fruits* . . . (274). To suggest that our qualities have a life of their own, like trees (594), seems to me hardly less original.

Artifice is often suggested by use of physical works of man, buildings, statues, hostelries, cosmetics, veils. Features of health and sickness of body are brought in, never obtrusively, to describe the mind: fever, medicine, diet, meat, even physical evacuation (which was removed before publication) (239; cf. H 141).

Twice the artist risks comparison of a quality of conduct with an actual person. The fool of Athens appears in 92 and 588, the Doge of Venice in 77: this seems to refer to a remark of Mazarin. We cannot perhaps at this distance of time tell which were dead and which were live metaphors. To speak of 'virtues on the *frontiers* of which lies . . . indolence' is perhaps in 1680 to paint a picture. (This, 512, he never published.)

9. The Tyrannical Self

It is time to look more closely at the most recurrent factor in the analysis of human behaviour, a factor we may define as the persistence in all conduct of self-interest. Many have judged LR by this alone. They have asked if he were right or wrong in suggesting the constant defeat of altruism by egoism. Few have gone on to ask—Prévost Parado lis a notable exception—what LR was actually saying, and meaning, and with what concepts he was working. To begin with, he uses, in the realm of self-interest, not any single term, but several, which do not seem to be entirely synonymous. Systematic analysis of LR's actual attitude is only possible if we submit these terms to exact scrutiny. The words we should watch are perhaps these: *intérêt, amour-propre, gloire, orgueil.* Maybe we should keep in mind the Maximes concerning *vanité* also, but without imposing any restricting definition until we are sure what is meant and referred to. We must take particular care that we operate with concepts of the seventeenth century and not with later connotations of the same words.

By *gloire* LR seems to understand that desire for reputation, for fame or for praise, for standing high in the opinion of others, which, for instance, makes men brave in battle, which inspires them to play a fine role: *certaines personnes aspirent à la gloire d'une belle douleur* (233). It is the temperament and attitude of the man who is *glorieux*, anxious for his reputation (141). Monsieur, the King's brother, tried to have it both ways, to be admired and familiar. This we learn from the *Mémoires* (Éd.

Pléiade, p. 80). This is the quality which has made men claim to despise death: . . . *ne pouvant éterniser leur vie, il n'y avait rien qu'ils ne fissent pour éterniser leur réputation, et sauver du naufrage ce qui n'en peut être garanti.* Note the image of shipwreck, closely followed in this Maxime (which is really a reflection and no epigram) by that of the hedge hiding soldiers from cross-fire: from a distance it looks like real protection, but when actually reached it is found to be of little help. Such are many of our desires when we are faced with the actual approach of death: *la gloire de mourir avec fermeté, l'espérance d'être regretté, le désir de laisser une belle réputation* . . . (504). This quality of *gloire* is seen as an offshoot or by-product of *amour-propre*, which in some men leads to love of money and in others to love of reputation or of pleasure: *Il a de différentes inclinations, selon la diversité des tempéraments, qui le tournent et le dévouent tantôt à la gloire, tantôt aux richesses, et tantôt aux plaisirs.* . . .

This is clearly not far from what we call, and what LR also calls, pride. *L'orgueil*, he says, is equal in all men (35); it is often the motive behind our maintaining unusual or unpopular opinions, a reaction to our inability to secure the best places, an assurance against being put at the back: *on trouve les premières places prises dans le bon parti, et on ne veut point des dernières* (234). This also is our motive for censuring those faults we do not have and excusing those we do have (462). This robs us of the true perception of things and blinds us both to our own condition and to its remedy. We have only to compare No. 585 with some words from the prefatory *Discours* of 1665 to see that this attitude stems from a close reading of Montaigne and the Fathers, as the *Discours* admits: . . . *quand l'amour-propre a séduit le cœur, l'orgueil aveugle tellement la raison, et répand tant d'obscurité dans ses connaissances, qu'elle ne peut juger du moindre de nos mouvements, ni former d'elle-même aucun discours assuré pour notre conduite* (Éd. Pléiade, p. 397). The way pride works out in conduct is contrary to what we might expect: we are forced to pride ourselves on jealousy, of which in secret we are ashamed (472). It produces in us that anger which can only be called madness (601). It forces us to simulate humility, so that even when we forswear vanity we lose nothing by doing so (33, 254). At times pride seems even to tire of mask and pretence and brazenly appears as *fierté*. I do not think that LR repeated this distinction between the two closely related terms. His removal of it after 1665 suggests that either he or others thought it perhaps over-subtle: *L'orgueil, comme lassé de ses artifices et de ses différentes Métamorphoses, après avoir joué tout seul tous les personnages de la Comédie humaine, se montre avec un visage naturel, et se découvre par la fierté; de sorte qu'à proprement parler, la fierté est l'éclat et la déclaration de l'orgueil* (568). Let us note that the tone of the reflections on pride is not that of a moralist anxious to condemn, but that of a dispassionate observer, concerned only to describe correctly what happens. In one place LR even suggests that he looks on pride as a gift of nature, intended like other physical features to make us happier, in this case by kindly concealing from us our shortcomings. Again it may be significant that the first published form of the reflection had to be toned down: *La nature, qui a si sagement pourvu à la vie de l'homme par la disposition admirable des organes du corps, lui a sans doute donné de l'orgueil pour lui épargner la douleur de connaître ses imperfections et ses misères* (36. A-text given in Éd. Pléiade, p. 773).

The term *intérêt* seems to have little to do with one's opinion of oneself. 'Self-interest' may be a passable trans-lation, so long as we remember that it denotes no con-scious thought or design, but something unconscious, innate, a part of our physical constitution which drives us to actions and words by which we stand to gain. *Intérêt* activates both virtues and vices. The famous epigram comparing it to a sea, in which our virtues are overwhelmed as rivers are when entering the ocean, makes no suggestion of our evil intention. It suggests rather, in the manner of Machiavelli's reflections on political man, that we rarely have time for virtue, being so beset by the necessity of self-assertion, this again not by design but as a biological accompaniment of being alive in a community. This comes close, as we have said, to the starting-point of Hobbes.

What might seem a merely cynical reflection could thus be more truly described as a clinical observation in such a Maxime as 305, which first appears in 1671: *L'intérêt, qu'on accuse de tous nos crimes, mérite souvent d'être loué de nos bonnes actions.* To a casual eye there might seem to be little difference between this quality and what we think of as *amour-propre*. So it may be significant that LR did distinguish not only the one from the other, but the singular from the plural. Where Mme de Sablé, for instance, refers to *les intérêts*, LR prefers the singular (see her Maxime No. 29, quoted Éd. Pléiade, p. 480). In one astonishing outburst, which he never consented to publish, he defined *intérêt* as '*l'âme de l'amour-propre*' and described in violently physical terms the latter as dormant and inert unless and until 'animated' by the chance approach of *intérêt*. Nowhere else do I recall so vivid a picture, not of the truth so much as of the almost instinctive sense (which seems to have obsessed LR) of the human person as an idle machine which is galvanized by the passions, or by anything that affects its survival. We have to wait until Balzac's *Avant-Propos* to the *Comédie humaine*, in 1846, before we meet another similar expression of the conviction that *la passion fait toute l'humanité.*

L'intérêt est l'âme de l'amour-propre, de sorte que comme le corps, privé de son âme, est sans vue, sans ouïe, sans connaissance, sans sentiment et sans mouvement, de même, l'amour-propre séparé, s'il le faut dire ainsi, de son intérêt, ne voit, n'entend, ne sent et ne se remue plus. De là vient qu'un même homme, qui court la terre et les mers pour son intérêt, devient soudainement paralytique pour l'intérêt des autres; de là vient ce soudain assoupissement et cette mort que nous causons à tous ceux à qui nous contons nos affaires; de là vient leur prompte résurrection lorsque, dans notre narration, nous y mêlons quelque chose qui les regarde; de sorte que nous voyons, dans nos conversations et dans nos traités, que dans un même moment, un homme perd connaissance et revient à soi, selon que son propre intérêt s'approche de lui, ou qu'il s'en retire. (510.)

This passionate passage should prevent us asking, as Vauvenargues asked, whether LR made any distinction between the words for *amour-propre*. Either he was using words loosely, or we have not read him closely. Perhaps we have missed the point because it is so plain. No more, perhaps, than that LR felt he needed two words to describe activities which to him were different. If we cannot mark the difference by two words which are not synonyms, then that may be due to the inadequacy of language. LR certainly speaks of *amour-propre* as of something more than a quality of our existence, almost a tendency or a feature of our constitution which activates a quality. This tendency is not what we term self-interest, it is nearer to self-preservation, which may be only another aspect of self-interest. It would seem to come roughly, as we say, to the same thing as self-interest, but an artist of the quality of LR is not likely to be handling words roughly, but delicately. Might we say that the quality of self-interest can be envisaged from several aspects, those, I suggest, which involve the human person in action, towards certain objects, aims, all of which turn out to have the single purpose (though not the conscious purpose) of self-advantage? *Amour-propre* is much more than this, it is a tendency of the whole being to look within, to worship self, to actuate, indeed, self-interest. It is not a quality of action nor of the human person. It is rather at a deeper level, the quality of personality, the nature of man in society, a basic determinant which acts through self-interest, but which must not be equated with it. So it is referred to in different language. It is defined as '*amour de soi, et de toutes choses pour soi*'. It is never thought of as only in some people, or active merely at intervals. It is that feature of man that accompanies all living, *dont toute la vie n'est qu'une grande et longue agitation*. The things LR has to say about this love of self go far beyond what he attributes to self-interest. He speaks in relation to it, and no doubt thinking of contemporary fiction, of 'idolatry' and of 'undiscovered countries', that is of something which is a kind of religion; he called it, though not for publication, the real God of fallen humanity. He spoke of it as vast in extent and in complexity, undiscovered, a mirage that gives us a good view of ourselves whatever others may say to flatter or to blame us. |30857|

Amour-propre played such a major role in his own thinking, and forced itself so violently on his capacity of expression, that it inspired him to write what may well be one of the most eloquent pages in the French language. These words stood at the head of the first edition of his *Réflexions*, and were removed from all subsequent editions in his lifetime. There is some suggestion that he was piqued at the criticism which he heard about them, and that he was particularly wounded by the word '*galimatias*'. The term is harsh but understandable, especially if they are re-read in the context in which they first appeared, Sercy's anthology of prose and verse in 1660. Among the *précieux* conceits and superficial graces of that volume the brief and pregnant sentences which we now read under No. 563 stand out, as John Buchan once said of Calvin's church at Geneva, 'as a power-house among tombs'. What to readers of *galanterie* in 1660 appeared

as words without meaning we can see to have been words
out of context, as if passages from Bossuet had been
printed among madrigals. Seen in the whole context of
LR's work, and in the still larger context of that critique
of life which was offered by the French classical *moralistes*,
these pages are full of meaning, but that meaning is poetic,
mysterious, intuitive rather than facile or 'polite'.

Yet in certain features LR can only describe things as
his age and society described them, that is by analogy.
For him *amour-propre* is a restless force, always active,
never satiated; it needs and procures nourishment, as
bees do from flowers. As it is insatiable, so it is incalculable, protean in its metamorphoses, as complex as the
mystery of alchemy. As LR describes its activities we
read of something animate, alive, making us think of
a beast, hiding in dark places, in recesses of incredible
depth and obscurity:

On ne peut sonder la profondeur, ni percer les ténèbres de
ses abîmes; là il est à couvert des yeux les plus pénétrants; il y
fait mille insensibles tours et retours; là il est souvent invisible
à lui-même; il y conçoit, il y nourrit et il y élève, sans le
savoir, un grand nombre d'affections et de haines; il en forme
de si monstrueuses que, lorsqu'il les a mises au jour, il les
méconnaît, ou il ne peut se résoudre à les avouer. . . .

This parent of monsters so unnatural that it cannot avow
its paternity is hidden in night and darkness, liable to
gross error, to fantastic misconceptions of its own nature,
yet gifted with the sharpest sight for anything that can
threaten or harm it. The quintessence of instability, it is
never the same, never consistent, content to undergo im-
mense trouble and labour for what will profit it nothing,
to counterfeit its enemies and to work for its own ex-
tinction in one form that it may rise in another, its sole
care being to persist and survive:

Il vit partout et il vit de tout, il vit de rien; il s'accommode
des choses, et de leur privation; il passe même dans le parti

des gens qui lui font la guerre, il entre dans leurs desseins,
et ce qui est admirable, il se hait lui-même avec eux, il conjure
sa perte, il travaille même à sa ruine; enfin il ne se soucie que
d'être et pourvu qu'il soit il veut bien être son ennemi.

To the taste of literary Paris in 1665 this was indeed
unintelligible, 'moonshine', unrelated, and not immediately relatable, to anything specific. The temper of
Sercy's readers was the reverse of visionary, and this
whole description is a vision, of dantesque proportions,
born as from a world of dream. We can see that *intérêt*
was a word too commonplace and prosaic to convey
what LR had to say. Prévost-Paradol seems to me rightly
to describe it as a vision of being, divorced from con-
siderations both of speculation on the one hand and of
morality on the other, constantly appealing to two forces
as yet unrecognized in polite letters (and in philosophy)
to the mysteries of the unconscious and to the analysis
of human nature divorced from, or rather untouched by,
ethical consideration. This too has its counterpart in
Hobbes and in later political thinkers. Prévost-Paradol
suggests that LR discovered the dynamic principle of
existence in all men, a *principe de vie, de l'être et de la
tendance à persévérer dans l'être*, something in fact pre-
ethical, almost animal, biological, something that a Freud
might have written had he lived in an age that was without
the tools or the language of a science of the unconscious.

Any complete picture of LR's notion of *amour-propre*
would have to include many reflections in which the
term is not used, such as the comment on what appears
to be disinterested plainness of manner or dress: *La
simplicité affectée est une imposture délicate* (289), or the gloss
on our self-love being greater than any praise can be:
*Quelque bien qu'on nous dise de nous, on ne nous apprend rien
de nouveau* (303).

The general opinion has perhaps been right in regard-
ing *amour-propre* as LR's main doctrine, his key to

human behaviour. The mistake is to think it a simple key, a catchword that accounts for all actions, however low or selfish. It is in fact a most complex conception, a new and untried and vaguely outlined contribution to the study of behaviour. Cynical it may seem to be, but cynicism cannot account for the imaginative power of No. 563. The note of pessimistic confidence present in the sharper and shorter Maximes is quite absent from this great outburst. Instead we find throughout a tone of respect as in the presence of mysterious forces, of something to be divined rather than discerned. LR would seem thus to be feeling his way towards some new angle of vision, some way of describing afresh the kind of behaviour which is usually thought of as unworthy, discreditable, immoral. It is striking that, although he was writing within a Jansenist circle, that is, one in which condemnation of conduct was natural, his tone is one of description rather than one of judgement. Nicole, and even Pascal, write about *amour-propre* with real abhorrence, as of a sin. LR seems more detached, more concerned patiently to uncover layers of behaviour not generally perceived, mineral deposits, one might say. Adam Smith will write with similar detachment of the self-interest of the tradesman.

In 1665 the novelty of such an exploratory attitude to conduct was such that LR, who as a writer seems to have been nervous and fearful of criticism, may well have agreed with his critics and decided that his reflections were possibly wide of the mark. He never republished his long *morceau*, and as far as is known never tried the same type of writing again as he had tried in 1659. None of his surviving *Réflexions diverses* attempts so wide a range of inquiry into a '*principe de vie*'. But as we survey his work we can discern, I suggest, the centrality of this *morceau*. It is the key to the rest of his writing, to those elements that his own disappointing

career does not fully explain. This picture of behaviour
suggests that all his reflections are fragments of an
anthropology. Seventeenth-century man is here seen
as a creature more impotent than wicked, as impotent
to do good rather than intent to do evil. He is described
as cruel not out of natural ferocity but for self-preservation
(604), as confessing his sins to gain the advantage of
being well thought of (609). Such an angle of observation would see in a grand funeral, as St. Augustine and
Montaigne had suggested, signs of the vanity of the
living rather than of honour paid to the dead. We should
read his Maxime, in view of the illustrious predecessors
whom he certainly knew, as intended to be not so much
an original observation as a part of his picture.

That picture is more interesting than that of any other
moraliste of his age. It seems to owe more to the camp and
the battlefield than to the drawing-room, but it has this
feature of salon conversation, that it suggests complexity
of behaviour which at first sight could be dismissed as
simple. Usually the behaviour is not judged or despised;
it is described, with a sense of the nuances and the variety
of situation one would expect to find in the *Mémoires* of
a Retz. Bravery, for instance, is neither despised nor
praised: it is noted as being different with varying
circumstance. LR is concerned not with the fact of
bravery but with the factors present in its actual exercise:
the care for safety, for reputation, the desire to avoid
censure, the influence of such factors as the time of day
or the type of weapon. Some men fear small things, and
some great things. Some are brave with a sword but not
with a gun. All men are less brave in the dark. All men
would be more brave if they were certain to survive the
battle (215).[1]

---

[1] The only author in whom I find this kind of penetration is André
Malraux, recalling his father's experience of gas warfare in 1915: 'Si je
crois que j'ai une chance, même infime, je suis courageux; mais si je sais

Once established, the inquiry runs on cynical lines, commenting on those features which either go unnoticed or which one would hope are not present in one's own case. We can understand the attraction of this in any discussion group. No wonder that its first audience found in it '*beaucoup d'esprit, peu de bonté, et force vérités que j'aurais ignorées toute ma vie, si l'on ne m'en avait fait apercevoir*' (Éd. Pléiade, p. 691). Gratitude, for example, brings reward: it increases trade. It also gives pleasure, and pride, the pride both of granting a grace and of receiving one. The way to attain power is to look honest; we call this hypocrisy, but it is at least an avowal that certain ends can only be attained by virtuous behaviour, so that we might speak of it (we can hear the suggestion being made within an intimate circle) as a compliment which vice pays to virtue (218).

Anyone who so observes men and affairs must seem biased, and must find it hard to avoid suspicion of good motives. So he will note that men are brave and women are chaste for other reasons than their natural possession of qualities we call bravery and chastity. Actions good and bad appear increasingly, as this scrutiny proceeds, as amalgams and not as pure qualities, as composed not at all of what is conformed to the nature of any person, but as imposed in a world of chance upon persons forced to defend and assert themselves. We can watch this process of analysis as LR reads history. What, he seems to ask, are the 'other factors' in a great action? Did Caesar fight Antony because of ambition to be master of the world? Or because one was jealous of the other? Montaigne had taught LR that a great occasion is an inscrutable thing. And the so-called great occasion has also those features seen in what most of us manage to do on a small occasion. We must not assume that

du fond du cœur que je ne l'ai pas, il n'y a plus de courage qui tienne' (*Les Noyers de l'Altenburg*, 1948, p. 179).

heroes are above the battle; they are probably very
like other men. The grand attitude, the assumption that
a principle can be asserted intact in the rough and tumble
of life, these are the target of many of LR's pungent observations. The point of view is often close to that of
Molière. The desire for frankness is natural and bound
to be defeated in fact. An Alceste may demand, as if
proclaiming a principle,

> qu'en toute rencontre
> Le fond de notre cœur en nos discours se montre,

but the absurdity of his attitude is that in cold fact we
expect this neither from others nor from ourselves: *Ce
qui nous empêche d'ordinaire de faire voir le fond de notre cœur
à nos amis, n'est pas tant la défiance que nous avons d'eux que
celle que nous avons de nous-mêmes* (315).

Both writers show this quality (which may well be a
feature of classicism) of preferring to abstract notions
of conduct the awareness of the checks and limits imposed on the notional by the actual, this sense of what
has been called '*l'échec*'. Chance, events, circumstances,
these are too much for us, and will not allow us to deploy
our qualities at their fullest: *La fortune et l'humeur gouvernent le monde* (435). We are, in addition, ignorant of our
real selves, of our actual power: *Nous n'avons pas assez de
force pour suivre toute notre volonté* (42), and *Il s'en faut bien
que nous connaissions toutes nos volontés* (295). So men in
society are beleaguered men, as the prefatory Discours
of the first edition expressed it, hindered and hemmed in
by chance and mood and the necessity of self-preservation
in a hostile world.

Yet all this working-out of self-interest is not a pity.
It is a condition of social living, and it is an advantage.
Social security, as Hobbes was to say so powerfully, is
only to be had at this price. If we could do as we would,
we should be tyrants each to the other: *l'amour-propre rend*

les hommes idolâtres d'eux-mêmes, et les rendrait les tyrans aes autres, si la fortune leur en donnait les moyens. It was probably LR's own experience of civil war that made him see this so clearly. He had seen how licence bred licence, how men were released in war from the bondage of convention: . . . *sans cette crainte, qui retient l'homme dans les bornes des biens que sa naissance ou sa fortune lui a donnés, pressé par la violente passion de se conserver, il ferait continuellement des courses sur les autres* (H 37). Or again, still closer perhaps to actual experience, as the memoirs of the time suggest it: *Rien n'est si contagieux que l'exemple, et nous ne faisons jamais de grands biens, ni de grands maux, qui ne produisent infailliblement leurs pareils. L'imitation d'agir honnêtement vient de l'émulation, et l'imitation des maux vient de l'excès de la malignité naturelle, qui étant comme tenue en prison par la bonté, est mise en liberté par l'exemple* (H 46).

10. The Problem of the *Réflexions diverses*

～✺～

AMONG LR's manuscripts was found a series of nineteen separate *réflexions*, each a page or more in length. Seven of these were published in the eighteenth century, and all of them in the nineteenth. The manuscripts from which they were taken have now both disappeared, so we have only their first editors' notes and summaries to go upon. A recently discovered copy seems to offer a more complete text than that so far known. Since 1731 they have been accepted as by LR, and no modern evidence has emerged to suggest the contrary. We must therefore treat them as his work, although we can know almost nothing for certain as to their date and destination.

Of these nineteen *réflexions* two (6 and 12) are said to have been erased, presumably by LR himself. Mystery and uncertainty surround this small body of writing. The only thing certain about it is fortunately what matters most, and that is its content. It does in fact give us a valuable glimpse into LR's attitude in the later years of his life. This much we can say, since the *Réflexions* quote the text of several published Maximes, mostly from the fourth and fifth editions, and they mention events occurring as late as 1678, and thus suggest that LR was at work on them within a year or so of his death.

The tone of these pages is quite different from that of the *Maximes*. They are relaxed, not at all cynical, and much more positive than are the *Maximes*. They seem to fit the reconsideration of 'salon topics', if one may call them so, by one whose views are known and need not be defended. Indeed, they are written with such studied moderation, with what would now be called such understatement, that their stylistic merits have not been noticed. We find if we study them in detail that the emphases which made the notoriety of the *Maximes* are not denied or contradicted: they are expressed in a relaxed and mellow context.

The matter of these *Réflexions* is more restricted than that of the *Maximes*. All of them deal with subjects which could be, and no doubt were, discussed in a salon. They avoid the dramatic, the startling, the search for epigram. They cover the main headings of serious conversation in intellectual circles of late seventeenth-century Paris. They exalt the art of conversation itself, which they envisage, not as a social pastime but, in the sense of Montaigne, as a social approach to the truth. They consider the nature of wit and taste, the judgements which are called for by the existence of great men, past and present, and by the occurrence of great events. They discuss illness and other problems of old age.

If they are read, not as an addendum to a famous work, but with careful consideration of composition and expression, that is to say if they are read in their own right, I think it is clear that they are the work of a great writer. Not only so, but they are unique, in their time. No other French writer has considered the problems of which they speak with such calmness, such objectivity, such moderation. They bear marks of the outlook of their author: great knowledge of men, experience of society both in war and peace, acceptance of the main assumptions of the French aristocracy (such as aversion to individualism and to pedantry). But these assumptions do not prevent their author from exploring the bases of social intercourse. They thus form an involuntary commentary on the world of *Le Misanthrope*. The fact of society is here considered at the same deep level as it is in Molière's play. This writing is classical in its sobriety and at the same time particular in its limitation to actual events. It corrects our assumption that the French aristo-cracy moved in a narrow world; it shows that among subjects of polite conversation could be, not only the marks of polite behaviour, but the revolutions accom-plished by Cromwell and Masaniello.

It is time that we tried to find out the attitudes behind this writing. It is not surprising to find a French aristo-crat stating, for example, that the art of war is more illustrious than the art of poetry. But it is surprising to find him saying this in order to suggest that Virgil is not inferior to Epaminondas, and that each was great within his own sphere. These are not unrelated observations: they suggest a serious attempt to work through to a proper notion of a quality common to different things. Two country houses as different as Liancourt and Chan-tilly have this quality in common. The cruelty of a child is no less cruel than that of the King of Spain. The generosity of rulers who bestow kingdoms is no more generous than that of the widow giving her mite (Pléiade 2 misses the biblical allusion here, and so the whole point of the *réflexion*). If we ask what brings these disparate comparisons together, on one level, we find it is not so much an idea as the style. The same words are used in the different cases, words designed to probe the quality without regard to size or 'importance'. The key word is *effacer*, used eight times. *Deux sujets de même nature peu-vent être différents, et même opposés . . . cependant, parce que leurs qualités sont vraies, elles subsistent en présence l'un de l'autre, et ne s'effacent point par la comparaison.* This word *effacer* is used by all the French classical poets, with a suggestion of regret, of something crossed out, caused not to be:

Je vous rappelle un songe effacé de votre âme
(*Mithridate*, 204).

It is defined and recognized by its contraries: *se maintenir*, *subsister*. The *réflexion* composed by these oppositions and affinities is in fact much the same sort of composition as it had been in the famous volume of 1665, too short for an essay, too long for an epigram, a series of suggestions, something on the way to a prose poem.

The second *réflexion* is no less rich in stylistic suggestion. We may note the care with which LR fences off its subject by excluding friendship, the association of people who like each other. Quite different is that *commerce particulier que les honnêtes gens doivent avoir ensemble.* A Frenchman of all people is likely to take for granted the need for general social intercourse. This Frenchman, with the remorseless inquiry of the *Maximes* behind him, is acutely aware of the individualism that denies the essential social premise: *on se préfère toujours à ceux avec qui on se propose de vivre.* So he investigates the conditions which must pertain if society is to be a bearable relation. Again we have two sets of expressions which seem to strike a balance. Certain words suggest necessity, something imposed by the nature of things: *nécessaire . . . il faut . . . doivent . . . doit . . .,* etc. These seem to hold up the argument. So many things are necessary, because people are what they are, because they do not suit each other, they impede each other: *on incommode* (the formulation goes back to an early Maxime). The problem therefore is to bring positive force to bear in the opposite direction: *rendre la société commode . . . s'accommoder . . . ensemble. . . contribuer. . . être facile à excuser. . . éviter. . . essayer . . .,* etc. Surely these groups of expressions are not accidental. They seem to act as a kind of intellectual rhyme, bringing the *réflexion* back to its basic swing. They present us with the conclusion which Alceste, and with him all idealists, resents: *La complaisance est nécessaire.* On the other hand, they admit his case: *elle doit avoir des bornes, elle devient servitude. . . .* Politeness is here broken down, as it were, into its various forms, into all those *ménagements* which we need if we are to handle other people without giving offence. Intelligence is not enough; other qualities are required: *bon sens* ... *humeur* ... *égards* ... *confiance* ... *variété*, in other words, positive efforts to be of use, and to be unobtrusive, to share concerns and not to probe into privacy, tact, the right approach. People, like statues (going back to another Maxime), need to be seen from the favourable angle. We all have our viewpoint, from which we would wish to be seen: no man can stand being seen in all things as he is.

It is in fact impossible to dissect these *Réflexions* without becoming aware of the close study of social relations which they assume. Maximes are quoted in the course of the argument, effortlessly, as references to ground already gone over. Such writing is impossible to one who had not had personal and long experience of egoism, sharp practice, ingratitude; and their opposites, altruism, magnanimity, honour. The diagnosis imposed by events has probably been sharpened by a reading of the Third Book of Montaigne.

The third *réflexion* indeed makes explicit use of one of Montaigne's fundamental distinctions. In a great passage, opening his essay on Books (II. 10), Montaigne had suggested the risks of confusing those qualities with which we are naturally endowed and those qualities we acquire through education and society:

C'est ici purement l'essai de mes facultés naturelles, et nullement des acquises; et qui me surprendra d'ignorance, il ne fera rien contre moi, car à peine répondrai-je à autrui de mes discours, qui ne m'en réponds pas à moi-même. . . . La science et la vérité peuvent loger chez nous sans jugement, et le jugement y peut aussi être sans elles; voire la reconnaissance de l'ignorance est l'un des plus beaux et plus sûrs témoignages de jugement que je trouve.

Contrary perhaps to our way of thinking, Montaigne would see judgement as a natural quality, our personal

sorting out, as it were, of the data supplied by reading
and by religion. LR applies this yardstick to society and
suggests that the natural runs the risk of being sub-
merged by the artificial. The charm of children is that
they are themselves; the error of grown-ups is to copy
others: *chacun veut être un autre*. This search for the natural
in an artificial society is in LR's hands an exciting quest.
Natural does not, as we might think, imply *informal*:
there is a natural way of walking at the head of a regi-
ment just as there is a natural way of taking a walk. But
dignities and distinctions corrupt and make us unnatural.
(Is he thinking of 'the insolence of office'?) We forsake
our natural bent in order to imagine ourselves distinguished: who knows how many middle-class women
ape the manners of a duchess?

All this imitation means forsaking what we could most
adequately be, which is ourselves: *on s'oublie soi-même, et
on s'en éloigne insensiblement*. The phrases even suggest that
LR has trained his ear to pick out the natural rhythm
of a person: *personne n'a l'oreille assez juste pour entendre
parfaitement cette sorte de cadence*. Here is the true spirit of
French classicism, its belief in balance, equilibrium, right
and due proportion of one's innate qualities to acquired
learning or social practice. This is the opposite of Rousseau: not the natural opposed to the social, but the
natural alongside the social.

The opening of the fourth *réflexion* suggests quite
strongly a date of composition relatively late in LR's
life. As in the fifth, he practically repeats a *sentence* which
in its first form had seemed harsh and bitter. Without
revoking it he seems to take the sting out of it, to place
it in a framework of mellow maturity. *Ce qui fait que si
peu de personnes sont agréables dans la conversation, c'est que
chacun songe plus à ce qu'il veut dire qu'à ce que les autres
disent*. Compare this with the text of Maxime 139; we
shall find the language almost identical, the content also.

Yet the tone is quite different. The one condemns; the other accepts. The one hits hard at the inattention and self-absorption (*égarement . . . précipitation . . .*) of the man who puts on an appearance of listening to somebody else. The other explores means of meeting the situation, of overcoming something that is bound to occur but which can be remedied. The one is negative, the other full of positive suggestions, such as avoiding points of difference, praising where possible, leaving the subject still open, not talking all the time, practising a tactful silence, and so on. This is to offer a sketch of conversation as an art, where omissions are of less consequence than positive intrusion of the self: . . . *laisser plutôt voir des négligences dans ce qu'on dit que de l'affectation.*

The difficult question of how much one should reveal in a conversation must have been discussed in many a salon. Should one, can one, keep private what one has in confidence heard? Can one resist the temptation of adding salt to a general observation by facts which will certainly be new and interesting? The rights of our friends, on our silence as on our speech, have their limits. If they complain of what we have not revealed to them, that is something we may remedy, whereas saying too much, letting out secrets, this may be irremediable.

A note in Pascal's hand suggests something so close to the seventh *réflexion* that it was possibly prepared for the same discussion. The subject is the effect of example. Good examples from the lives of great men may have bad effects, as also bad examples may persuade us to avoid evil. Both writers take the case of Alexander the Great. Pascal says that it offers excuse for drunkenness; LR is less sharp:

Combien la valeur d'Alexandre a-t-elle fait de fanfarons. Combien la gloire de César a-t-elle autorisé d'entreprises contre la patrie. . . . Tous ces grands originaux ont produit un nombre infini de mauvaises copies. Les vertus sont frontières des vices. . . .

We note the old skill in the phrasemaking, but why should such matters occupy serious people? The attraction of the subject is, I suggest, that it allows a critical spirit to play around, and play with, phenomena. We are shown men and deeds we are supposed to consider great. Does the matter end there? Is it just a question, as the moralists tell us, of copying the good and avoiding the bad? In actual fact this does not happen: *les exemples sont des guides qui nous égarent souvent.* Once launched on the world, a great quality, a deed, or a reputation may have consequences both immoral and incalculable. Is not LR working his way here to some existential view of history? He finds it too simple to think of great men just as examples; they are facts, they exist, we may make of them what we can.

The salon's preoccupation with love, the intellectual discussion of emotional effects, is the subject of five *réflexions* (6, 8, 9, 15, 17). The *réflexion* on the uncertainty of jealousy is a return to something which had fascinated LR by its terrible effects. Two of his early Maximes speak of the '*fureur*' caused by jealousy. The *réflexion* is calmer in tone, and almost playful in its linguistic juggling with something that resists our pressure and our power to tie down.

On cherche à s'attacher à une opinion et on ne s'attache à rien . . . on se travaille incessamment pour arrêter son opinion, et on ne la conduit jamais à un lieu fixe. Of this uncertainty Sisyphus is the apt image, the symbol of pointless striving: *on roule . . . on voit . . . on s'efforce . . . on l'espère . . . mais on n'y arrive jamais.* Time is here brought in to enforce lack of achievement. Our state of ignorance is a continuing state, exasperating in its failure to fix and grasp the sense of a pointless succession: *On est assujetti à une incertitude éternelle, qui nous présente successivement des biens et des maux qui nous échappent toujours.* Can prose be more closely knit than this, where words react on and support each other and all work in the same sense?

The subject does not always match the treatment. The *réflexion* on love and life (9), for example, is a rather laboured comparison of the three 'ages' of love to a lifespan of youth, maturity, and decline. The idea is in itself somewhat *précieux*, in its attempt to confer, upon arbitrary and forced metaphor, *la vieillesse de l'amour*, that sense of growth which we associate with a life. Yet it comes to life at the point where we might expect it to be most forced and unreal:

> . . . la joie n'est plus vive, on en cherche ailleurs que dans ce qu'on a tant désiré. Cette inconstance volontaire est un effet du temps, qui prend malgré nous sur l'amour comme sur notre vie; il en efface insensiblement chaque jour un certain air de jeunesse et de gaieté, et en détruit les plus véritables charmes; on prend des manières plus sérieuses, on joint des affaires à la passion; l'amour ne subsiste plus par lui-même, et il emprunte des secours étrangers.

Surely this again is fine writing, suggesting a Proustian probing into the invisible and the imperceptible. Was it perhaps one service rendered by the *précieux* movement to inspire descriptions (like 563) which to some seemed *galimatias* but which at moments stumbled on the vast undiscovered world of the unconscious and spoke of it in a manner which turned affectation into mystery?

Is not this the case with the pages on *les coquettes et les vieillards* (15)? What would seem to be a somewhat astringent meditation on *ce goût dépravé des coquettes pour les vieilles gens* suggests hyperbole in its picture of the practised flirt bringing the dead to life, and attaching, as in the *Amadis de Gaule*, dwarfs to her train. And this make-believe has its counterpart in the devastating realism of the picture of the old man, seeking comfort and pride in the apparent revival of his power to please.

> Il se persuade aisément qu'il est aimé, puisqu'on le choisit contre tant d'apparences; il croit que c'est un privilège de son vieux mérite, et remercie l'amour de se souvenir de lui dans

tous les temps. . . . Quel vieillard ne se rassure pas par des raisons si convaincantes, qui l'ont souvent trompé quand il était jeune et aimable? Mais pour son malheur il oublie trop aisément qu'il n'est plus ni l'un ni l'autre et cette faiblesse est de toutes la plus ordinaire aux vieilles gens qui ont été aimés. Je ne sais même si cette tromperie ne leur vaut pas mieux encore que de connaître la vérité : on les souffre du moins, on les amuse, ils sont détournés de la vue de leurs propres misères et le ridicule où ils tombent est souvent un moindre mal pour eux que les ennuis et l'anéantissement d'une vie pénible et languissante.

Contemporary writers could have worked up the conceit of the basic absurdity of old men in love. LR had himself done so in more than one Maxime. But only the great writer could set this against the backcloth, so to speak, of the miserable end of those whose days are no more than meaningless boredom.

Considered as language, the most remarkable perhaps of the *réflexions* on love is one which was possibly crossed out by its author. In view of his withdrawal of his pages on *amour-propre* we need not take this later condemnation of his own work too seriously. For here again we have a page such as no other classical author could write, but a classical page, explicitly probing the renewal of a hackneyed comparison. The *lieux communs* are neatly packed into a single sentence. The real matter is a quite new parallel, that of dying love (*un amour usé, languissant et sur sa fin*) with equatorial calm; no wind, and thus no chance of reaching the land within sight. The catalogue takes on the pitiless quality of actual exposure : sickness, lassitude, diversion that brings no comfort, boredom, monotony, life going on against our will : even desire loses point. It is the only passage in French that I could compare with Goethe's picture of the dead calm of love :

> Keine Luft von keiner Seite,
> Todesstille fürchterlich.

I think that the prose of the Frenchman can sustain the comparison:

> ... on voit la terre, mais on manque de vent pour y arriver; on se voit exposé aux injures des saisons; les maladies et les langueurs empêchent d'agir; l'eau et les vivres manquent ou changent de goût; on a recours inutilement aux secours étrangers; on essaye de pêcher et on prend quelques poissons, sans en tirer de soulagement ni de nourriture; on est las de tout ce qu'on voit, on est toujours avec ses mêmes pensées, et on est toujours ennuyé; on vit encore et on a regret à vivre; on attend des désirs pour sortir d'un état pénible et languissant, mais on n'en forme que de faibles et d'inutiles.

Is it not strange that a writer of great power such as La Bruyère should have been so praised for his accumulation of precise details, and that writing such as this should go unnoticed? Precision of concrete detail such as gesture and furniture is in fact something La Bruyère may have learned from these accumulated impressions, this plastic power of writing, which are both of LR's own age and also full of suggestion even after three hundred years.

As if to show that *précieux* gallantry might grow stale, the *Réflexions* return to some of the main themes of the *Maximes*, such as the workings of chance, the nature of intelligence, the biological aspects of man. This last topic brings him (in No. 11) on to the same ground as La Fontaine. He makes out a case for considering men as animals. The whole range of the animal kingdom is brought in to enforce the point that so-called human qualities are savage, cunning, vain, pompous, natural. Once launched, the artist in LR seems to delight in making his picture as varied and as complete as is the variety of creation itself. Birds, cats, snakes, spiders . . . the Noah's Ark fills up, and by speed of accumulation the artificial impression of the catalogue is avoided. It is, in fact, almost the subject-matter of the *Fables*, yet at no point is the comparison so precise as to suggest conscious imitation. True, La Fontaine published his second collection (Books VII to XI) in 1678, and may well have incited LR to this *réflexion* or actually discussed it with him. But I cannot find any detail in it of which one could say that LR could not have thought of it independently of the poet. To use this *réflexion*, therefore, as has been done, to determine the dating of LR's later writing seems to me both unwise and unnecessary. LR may well have been inspired, as Professor Truchet suggests, by Charles Le Brun's lecture of 1671, or by the French translation of an Italian Renaissance manual of physiognomy in which plates showed animal and human heads side by side (see *Maximes*, ed. Truchet, p. 204).

Much more important than the date of the *réflexion* is what redeems it from monotony, the underlying persuasion that it is dangerous to disregard the animal part of man. The Pascalian concepts of '*la bête*' and '*la misère de l'homme*' are akin to this writing. Where Pascal is brief and general, LR is precise and particular, as indeed was Molière in *Tartuffe*. Some of us were brought up to consider as *not* classical such touches as the comparison of men to moles, who live out of sight, to horses, who work till they drop, to swallows, fine weather birds, to crocodiles, who shed tears in order to make sure of their prey. The final case is unexpected, as so often with this writer: *Et combien d'animaux qui sont assujettis parce qu'ils ignorent leur force.*

It is no surprise to the student of the *Maximes* to find a *réflexion* dealing with chance, but again its spirit seems other than that of Maxime 153, which it quotes almost exactly: *La nature fait le mérite et la fortune le met en œuvre.* It pursues the independent line of considering cases of nature and chance working together to produce the perfect work of art. Alexander, Caesar, and Cato are seen as prototypes of contemporaries, Condé and Turenne. These pages can hardly have been written before Condé's retirement in 1676, a year after the death of Turenne, and the comparison, as Bossuet's *Oraison funèbre* bears witness, must have been a favourite theme. The Maxime had suggested that greatness does not come from merit alone. Perhaps we have misread this by imputing to it the cynicism found elsewhere in the *Maximes*. An epigram would naturally make the point sound sharper than it would in the context of reasoned reflection. Yet both may spring from the impulse to reach a true distinction between the spheres of character and circumstance.

Another theme of the *Maximes* elaborated in the *Réflexions* is the nature of wit. The epithets applied to the term *esprit* are assembled in *RD* 16: *grand, bel, bon, adroit, fin, utile, brillant, moqueur*, and so on. It is difficult to say whether the unusual twist at the end, distinguishing between the various kinds of saying which arouse attention and admiration, is really subtle, or just one more case of the rage for analysis, for the *distinguo* that seems to lie behind all *précieux* writing. Yet LR has the last word in admitting that when it was said of anyone, as the king said of Racine, that he had *beaucoup d'esprit*, it was not possible to know exactly what was meant.

As the *Maximes* ended with a meditation on death, so the *Réflexions* seem to culminate in the pages on '*la retraite*' (*RD* 19; in Truchet's edition, No. 18). LR here seems to interpret this title (for himself, of course, in the first place) almost literally, asking what is involved in withdrawal from one's kind: men, like animals, when in fullness of years they are overtaken by a change in looks, in mood, and in physical constitution, avoid company. Seeking, still in the *précieux* manner, to avoid confusion of like and unlike, to make proper distinctions, LR pursues his quest as to what exactly is changed when a person gets old. So many things become impossible, so many avenues no longer open, avenues to greatness, to pleasure, to fame. So many things change:

friends die, reputation declines, the faculties diminish: *chaque jour leur ôte une partie d'eux-mêmes*. In such a state, what does one see ahead but more anxiety, illness, decline—*chagrins, maladies, abaissement*. Novelty has gone, and so has focus, that point *d'où il leur convient de voir les objets, et d'où ils doivent être vus*. This being so, old men receive from other men only indifference, or scorn. They therefore withdraw from human contacts to the inanimate things which may still please: buildings, crops, books, accounts. Wise men turn to religion, most men to brooding on their disabilities and to such relief as they may still find in absence or diminution of pain. The final picture is one of increasing insensibility:

> ... la nature, défaillante et plus sage qu'eux, leur ôte souvent la peine de désirer; enfin ils oublient le monde, qui est si disposé à les oublier; leur vanité même est consolée par leur retraite, et avec beaucoup d'ennuis, d'incertitudes et de faiblesses, tantôt par piété, tantôt par raison, et le plus souvent par accoutumance, ils soutiennent le poids d'une vie insipide et languissante.

The power and rhythm of this language seem to me remarkable. The text is uncertain: the manuscripts differ at a crucial point. Yet it suggests great power to convey the physical complexities of a mood and a state of life. The balance is uncanny. On the one side are *ennuis, incertitudes* (or *inquiétudes*) and *faiblesses*. On the other, *piété, raison, accoutumance*. Fom this balance results the burden of life (the word *poids* recurs at the end of *RD* 17), of a life without savour, without energy, a life that does no more than persist.

To these *Réflexions* there is a postscript, which the most reliable contemporary manuscript, the only one, in fact, to give the full text, puts last of all. This is LR's attempt to sort out from the multitude of contemporary events those which deserved to be recorded and remembered. So many things happen in a lifetime that the mind fails to distinguish—again the desire to make distinct some things from other things—the truly unusual. LR presents thirteen such events, the most singular that his age can show. As a man of his age, an age which had little understanding of what we call history, he thinks that only the extraordinary is worth mention. The cases he selects all concern sovereignty, either of kings and queens, or of usurpers or despots. The broader view of a Voltaire, which discerns tendencies and forces, is never so much as hinted.

As in the old tragedy, what makes an event singular and memorable is reversal of fortune: *Marie de Médicis, reine de France . . . morte de misère et presque de faim.* This opening case might stand for all the others. *Ange de Joyeuse, duc et pair,* renounced the world but undertook two double journeys to Rome, on foot, to make his case: *la vanité dont il avait triomphé dans le milieu des grandeurs triompha de lui dans le cloître.* The Portuguese Duke of Braganza *fut déclaré roi contre sa propre volonté, et se trouva le seul homme de Portugal qui résistât à son élection.* A subject, Richelieu, made himself master of the State, to the point of executing the king's friends, yet died in his bed, a dictator of such power that he could leave a will which forced the king to obey him more blindly after death than in life. Reversal too in the most detailed and dramatic of all these 'events', that of the Grande Mademoiselle, grand-daughter of Henri IV, choosing at the age of 43 to wed Lauzun, forbidden to do so by the king. Lauzun, denied his elevation, loses his temper, breaks his sword in the Royal presence, insults Mme de Montespan and is imprisoned for life in Pignerol. Conversely, revolution, in Naples and in England, achieved in the first case by *un vendeur d'herbes* and in the second by *un lieutenant d'infanterie sans nom et sans crédit.* (Of Cromwell, as of Richelieu and the Duke of Braganza, LR is careful to record that they died in their beds, *paisible*.) Two cases of abdication, by the Queen of Sweden and the King of Portugal, were also noted by Pascal. Two cases of reversal of policy without due cause, offering what M. Truchet has called *une version officielle et française des événements*, close the series, except for a remarkable tail-piece, a reflection on the unheard-of vices of the age. It is brief and pungent, as if the author was concerned to say a last word in testimony to the fact that, in violent crime, the France he knew had surpassed even ancient Greece. Here, as so often before, he seems concerned to tear the veil from convention. The studied moderation of his usual style gives to this final judgement unusual force:

> Les vices sont de tous les temps, les hommes sont nés avec de l'intérêt, de la cruauté et de la débauche; mais si des personnes que tout le monde connaît avaient paru dans les premiers siècles, parlerait-on présentement des prostitutions d'Héliogabale, de la foi des Grecs et des poisons et des parricides de Médée?

Is it any wonder that Proust, when faced with the problem of portraying the vices of Charlus, could find among his amazingly wide reading no more forceful support than this forgotten sentence? (It is forgotten, apparently, even by his latest editors, who speak of it as a *maxime sans doute apocryphe* (Éd. Pléiade, III).)

What is one to say in sum of these penetrating and personal *Réflexions*? Chiefly, perhaps, that their mysterious origin and modest appearance—complete in only one manuscript, unpublished by the author—has led them to be treated by editors (with one exception) as an insignificant addendum to the main work. They are thus an unpretentious work, lacking all signs of parade or *réclame*. With classical sobriety LR probes the facts of life and society, and presents his findings as tentative, as hardly worth attention, as minor correctives to the scandalous book which has made him famous. But the touch of scandal has gone; the tone is rather that of modest expression of views which all reasonable men will share.

This is deceptive, and unfair. The studied restraint is itself a feature of fine writing, a classical feature. These apparently disconnected *Réflexions* offer, more satisfyingly perhaps than does any French writing of the later seventeenth century, some of the unspoken bases of aesthetic judgement. They go deeper than the *Art poétique*, they cover a greater range than the Prefaces of Racine or the occasional dicta of La Fontaine. The pedantry of Bouhours, as of Guez de Balzac, is here entirely absent. And they are classical. They do not deny artifice, in style or in behaviour. They are original in uncovering the bases common to both style and behaviour. Above all, they insist on the classical notion of truth, truth in nature, truth to nature, truth regarded as the natural within a civilized framework, as the maximum of nature which may be preserved by civilization. Their standards of judgements are seen in the recurrent appearance of words such as *juste, justesse, limites, mesure, propre*. They thus suggest an art of living, a refusal to consider the individual apart from those around him, as for example in this unspectacular sentence: *On ne saurait avoir trop d'application à connaître la pente et la portée de ceux à qui on parle* (*RD* 4); or in the even less remarkable '*membre de phrase*' in the preceding *réflexion*: *différemment mais toujours naturellement*. Whatever is considered, be it the standards of society or the examples of great men, the tool of measurement, the yardstick, so to say, is the same. It finds adequate expression in the course of a careful analysis of variation in taste:

Dans toutes ces différences de goûts que l'on vient de marquer, il est très rare, et presque impossible, de rencontrer cette sorte de bon goût qui sait donner le prix à chaque chose,

qui en connaît toute la valeur, et qui se porte généralement
sur tout: nos connaissances sont trop bornées, et cette juste
disposition des qualités qui font bien juger ne se maintient
d'ordinaire que sur ce qui ne nous regarde pas directement.
(*RD* 10.)

The implications of such a sentence as this are worth
some notice. One might say that the ideal, in life as in
art, is a question of taste, of proportion, of preserving
the right balance between the individual and the rest,
between one's own writing and the norm. The pre-
requisite, for doing right as for right expression, is the
same: a distrust of appearance and an effort to discern the
real factors of behaviour and of style. Beyond this, in
one sense, one cannot go: *C'est que les uns veulent paraître
ce qu'ils ne sont pas, les autres sont ce qu'ils paraissent.*

In such thinking the ideal is not a perfection of qualities, but a proportion, a suiting, a matching of behaviour
and style to the actual conditions and qualities which
real people possess. What lets us down, gives us away,
makes us unreal, is the rage to copy others, the effort to
suggest that we are other than we are: *On aime à imiter;
on imite souvent, même sans s'en apercevoir, et on néglige ses
propres biens pour des biens étrangers, qui d'ordinaire ne nous
conviennent pas.*

We may see what is involved by asking what this
critique of style is not. It is not in itself religious, although it springs from an Augustinian milieu and probably owed much to it. The characteristic emphases of
Port-Royal were, of course, well known to LR. Of the
Maximes Sainte-Beuve once wrote that *elles ne contredisent
en rien le christianisme, bien qu'elles s'en passent.* Here we
touch on a real achievement of French classicism, which
is rarely mentioned. They did not need to discuss or
to justify their religious position, because they could
assume it, and work out a secular point of vantage from
which they might scrutinize behaviour, a point of view

which need not be doctrinal, nor even expressed in religious terms, but which rests on a religious basis. Pascal applied a strictly religious and even biblical criterion to behaviour, but others of his circle did not feel the need to do this. The *Epigrammatum Dilectus* of 1659, which was the chief literary anthology of Port-Royal, expresses almost exactly LR's view of beauty (and I suggest of truth also) as we read it in the *Réflexions*:

Les choses sont belles lorsqu'elles s'accordent avec leur propre nature et avec la nôtre. La beauté réside donc dans un double rapport. Un rapport de l'objet avec lui-même, équilibre des parties, harmonie intérieure. Et un rapport de l'objet avec la nature de l'homme. (*Préface, apud* Adam, *Histoire de la litt. fr. au 17ᵉ siècle*, ii. 177.)

Nor would it be right to call this critique elaborated by LR a rational critique, except in the most general sense. It is more than intellectual, and it includes the social:

L'esprit . . . ne suffit pas seul pour nous conduire dans les divers chemins qu'il faut tenir. Le rapport qui se rencontre entre les esprits ne maintiendrait pas longtemps la société si elle n'était réglée et soutenue par le bon sens, par l'humeur, et par des égards qui doivent être entre les personnes qui veulent vivre ensemble. (*RD* 2.)

LR wrote in prose, and without didactic intention, so he was enabled to avoid both the pitfalls to which Boileau, for all his wit, fell a victim. He did not need to give advice, and he ran no risk of applying an intellectual critique to poetry. He was nearer in mind to the Boileau who translated Longinus, who was aware of the emotions and of the power of words. Some of his writing, for all its sobriety, may be thought to approach the sublime.[1]

---

[1] The word is not mine. It occurs in a private note by Sainte-Beuve: *Pour bien entendre LR il faut se dire que l'amour-propre dans ses replis de protée et ses métamorphoses prend parfois des formes sublimes* (*Mes Poisons*, p. 174). I think it is time that this aspect of LR's genius should be accorded the respect which the great critic gave to it.

It may be more important to stress the features that Boileau and LR have in common, rather than what separated them. Both men lay stress on truth: *le vrai seul est aimable* can apply to living as well as to writing. The first part of the line, though more doubtful, would still fit them both: *rien n'est beau que le vrai*. The first of the *Réflexions*, the abandoned Maxime 626 (which LR confessed (in 1663?) that he did not understand, but which he may well have come to agree with later), suggests the same view as that of Boileau. Put in simple terms this view is that anything we call beautiful or perfect convinces us by its truth, which means the exact correspondence between the nature and the exercise of that thing. Both to have made this clear and to have provided examples of it (in fable, comedy, tragedy, novel, letter, epigram, sermon) is perhaps the true glory of French classicism. Many kinds of writing show this, none as profoundly as the greater comedies of Molière. Their specifically comic element, which Molière himself called '*le ridicule*', is seen whenever a thing or a person is displayed as patently not what it was meant to be. *Le seigneur Harpagon est, de tous les humains, l'humain le moins humain.* Tartuffe overlooks the fact that *pour être dévot je n'en suis pas moins homme.* He forgets that he is totally, not just cerebrally, human. So does Alceste, who regrets that his love is not ruled by his reason. But when hit by adversity (a brilliant touch) he admits that we are all ignorant of what we really are: *ce grand aveuglement où chacun est de soi.* The same insight appears in the second *réflexion*: *on veut être averti jusqu'à un certain point, mais on ne veut pas l'être en toutes choses, et on craint de savoir toute sorte de vérités.*

If this critique is not religious, not rational in the Cartesian sense, how then shall we characterize it? I should be tempted to say it is 'pre-Enlightenment'. It is the high point of European awareness reached in the late seventeenth century. Has it been noticed that LR frequently admits, as in the quotation above, the limits of what we actually know, about the universe, about living, about ourselves? *Nos connaissances sont trop bornées.* This was so in every field, and thanks to the efforts of men like Richard Simon, Bayle, and Fontenelle, it was much less so by 1720. The way had been opened to a vast increase in human knowledge. But the attitude to that increase had been painfully elaborated throughout the preceding century. The development of scientific investigation which took place in the eighteenth century would not have been possible without, not only what is known as the 'scientific revolution', but also the sorting-out process of ideas perfected by the French classical writers. That process rested on the use of reason accompanied by a critique of reason. As Pascal put it: *Il faut avoir ces trois qualités, pyrrhonien, géomètre, chrétien soumis . . . elles s'accordent et se tempèrent.*

So that the proper formulation of the problem of the *Réflexions diverses* would seem to be rather different from the way in which it is usually put. Their date and relation to the *Maximes* are indeed uncertain, and may never be established. But that may not greatly matter. The real problem of the *Réflexions* is that of appreciating one of the most mature documents of the classical age.

11. Conclusion

JOUBERT is credited with the reflection, no doubt a sad comment on his own inability, that *heureux est l'écrivain qui peut faire un beau petit livre*. The small work which we have here tried to study has revealed complexities which one would not expect from apparently conventional comments on behaviour in a conforming society. To study these we have had to separate the artist from the thinker, and to retrace the work of both from the finished formulation back to the earliest drafts. This does not mean that the first draft is as important as the final one, except for the purposes of study, of precise investigation into the mind and the art of the author. But I think it may be said that study allows us to see more in a Maxime than we might have discovered unaided. An epigram which at first seems to dazzle yields on closer acquaintance a peculiar and durable pleasure. We read it, not as a flash in the pan or a lucky hit, but as a fine fusion of form and critical intelligence. Patient analysis allows us to surprise the marriage of novelty and profundity. There cannot have been many books which both Voltaire and Nietzsche went out of their way to praise.

Jean-Jacques affected to despise LR and *son triste livre*, because, like many readers before and after him, he could not get beyond the cynicism. The reason for this is clearer to us than it could be to him. To be buffeted by a society which is in turmoil and which you are acute enough to see through is bound to result in pronouncements which may easily be misinterpreted. Misfortune and insight, in the case of LR as in that of Swift, do not make for pleasant writing.

Perhaps Vigneul Marville, writing sixty years earlier than Rousseau, came nearer the mark: *Tout y est original, la matière et la forme.* Other contemporaries were not unmindful of the subtlety behind the metallic statements. The very title, said Huet, was a paradox: the word *maxime* suggests truths seen by the light of nature and known to all, whereas this book contained statements *découvertes par la méditation et les réflexions d'un esprit pénétrant et clairvoyant.* Far from being true, they were clearly biased. LR's own life prevented him from being fair, and his art tempted him to prefer elegance of expression to the truth: *l'auteur impute souvent un vice pour ne pas perdre une expression élégante et nouvelle . . . l'expression n'a pas été inventée pour l'accusation, mais l'accusation a été inventée pour y faire entrer l'expression.* The critic, no less than the artist whom he judges, may be concerned to be witty rather than truthful.

It is not the concern of these pages to deny the cynicism of LR. To do so would be to fly in the face of what is known of his public role as well as of the plain sense of his writing. But to judge the *Maximes*, as many have done, by their cynicism is to risk seeing nothing else, and for the attentive reader there is much else. A better critic than Huet, André Gide, was generous enough to disown his own first judgement: in his book on Dostoevsky, written in 1910, he had gone so far as to say of LR: *tout ce qu'il y a de contradictoire dans l'âme humaine lui échappe* (p. 182).

There is no need to deny what seems to be the plain fact, that LR had keener eyes for the presence of self-interest than for that of altruism, provided we admit that he was looking at a society in disruption and decline. The best answer to him, for those who wish the opposing point to be put, seems to me to have been given by Bourdaloue:

Si les libertins pouvaient être témoins de ce qui se passe en certaines âmes solidement chrétiennes et pieuses, s'ils voyaient la droiture de leur intention, la pureté de leurs sentiments, la délicatesse de leur conscience . . . ils auraient peine à les comprendre; ils en seraient étonnés, touchés, charmés, et bien loin de s'attacher comme ils font à tourner la piété en ridicule, ils en respecteraient, même jusque dans la fausse, les apparences, de peur de se tromper sur la vraie. (*Sermon sur l'injustice du monde*, in Bremond, *Histoire littéraire du sentiment religieux*, viii. 310.)

Yet even admitting the preacher to have been right, we must remember that LR, in his analysis of a sick society (and the circles in which LR moved were certainly corrupt), had clear-sighted contemporaries who agreed with him. A good example is Retz on Cromwell:

La maxime la plus véritable pour juger sainement des intentions des hommes est d'examiner leurs intérêts, qui sont la règle la plus ordinaire de leurs actions; et la politique la plus délicate ne rejette pas absolument les conjectures que l'on peut tirer de leurs passions, parce qu'elles se mêlent quelquefois assez ouvertement et qu'elles se coulent presque toujours insensiblement dans les ressorts qui donnent le mouvement aux affaires les plus importantes. Ceux qui sont persuadés que Cromwell n'a rompu avec le Roi Catholique que par la colère que lui donna la saisie de ses vaisseaux arrêtés, par représailles de ses voleries, dans les ports d'Espagne, seront aisément de cette opinion, qui aura toujours beaucoup plus de vraisemblance à l'égard de Cromwell que des autres politiques, parce qu'il est croyable que les fureurs dont il est agité occupent assez souvent dans son esprit le lieu destiné aux pures lumières de la raison. (*Remontrance au Roi*, 1657, Éd. Pléiade, p. 1010.)

One may even say that LR is writing within a constant French tradition. Montaigne shared many of his insights. Flaubert echoes his point of view: *Je cherche les vilains fonds* . . . (Corresp., i. 294). This tradition is that of the *moralistes*, writers less concerned to teach and prescribe than to observe and analyse. Montaigne could speak for them all when he said: *Les autres forment l'homme, je le recite* (III. 2). The insights of both men can usually be traced back to the reporting of actual events. Perhaps this was what Mandeville learned from LR: 'One of the greatest reasons why so few people understand themselves is that most writers are always teaching men what they should be, and hardly ever trouble their heads with telling them what they really are' (*Fable of the Bees*, introduction to 1723 edition).

That LR's penetration into behaviour and its motives found such powerful and adequate artistic expression can only be called one of the great successes of literature. The form of the epigram, impersonal, unattached, elusive, allusive, is one of the oldest of literary forms, and was admirably suited to the probings of a new morality. Some readers have been disconcerted by the discrepancy and disorder of the *Maximes*, by the way in which LR deliberately covered up his tracks in splitting up and separating Maximes dealing with the same subject. This is not personal pique; it is, as an acute student of the matter has recently commented,[1] the way Maximes should appear if they are to have their full effect of shock and surprise. This apparent disorder is the mark, strangely enough, of the classical artist, concerned that his investigations should not be tied to their origin or limited by other related statements, but should strike with maximum force readers who were accustomed to a more conventional way of thinking.

Finally, those who find the *Maximes* no more than pithy or bright have not reached their full savour. The paradox (in the very nature of the epigram) is that it sounds and looks final, metallic, absolute, closed. In fact it is a means of opening out its subject, of introducing new vision. It is not an end, but a beginning.

[1] J. Starobinski, in *NRF*, July and August 1966.

Index Nominorum

འགྲ

PRINTED IN GREAT BRITAIN
AT THE UNIVERSITY PRESS, OXFORD
BY VIVIAN RIDLER
PRINTER TO THE UNIVERSITY